Leading From the Top

Leading From the Top

Presidential Lessons in Issues Management

Dennis M. Powell

BEP

BUSINESS EXPERT PRESS

Leader in applied, concise business books

First published in 2023 by
Business Expert Press, LLC
222 East 46th Street, New York, NY 10017
www.businessexpertpress.com

ISBN-13: 978-1-63742-541-1 (paperback)
ISBN-13: 978-1-63742-542-8 (e-book)

Business Expert Press Human Resource Management and Organizational Behavior Collection

First edition: 2023

10 9 8 7 6 5 4 3 2 1

*To my wife Lisa who gave me the space to pursue my dreams;
my mother Mary for her unconditional love, and my friend
Peter Dougherty who put me on the path toward realizing
my dream of having my book published.*

Description

Leading From the Top is a journey through 90 years of American presidential history to glean lessons in issues management from those who dealt with the most complex issues, on the biggest stage and under the most intense scrutiny. Reading the book, you will learn why asking permission, reframing the issue, and knowing the length of your runway are all important components in successful issues management.

This book uses history to build on common knowledge to accelerate recall of the concepts presented. It looks at 15 presidents, from Franklin Roosevelt to Joe Biden, and examines one issue each managed. Each chapter ends by assessing success or failure through the lens of issues management consulting and providing succinct lessons that readers can draw from and apply to conflict resolution, problem-solving, and crisis management.

Leading From the Top is written for both aspiring and seasoned leaders to learn about or refine their issues management approaches, as well as the reader who is interested in a different way to assess our presidents. This said, the book is not written to be prescriptive on any of the issues presented, but simply to provide perspective and tools to use to do your own assessments going forward.

Keywords

leadership; management; communications; problem-solving; crisis management; strategy; conflict resolution; assessment; Presidents of the United States; issues management

Contents

Testimonials

"Dennis Powell has done a masterful job of bringing insight into leadership using Presidents from Roosevelt to Biden as his foundation. He marries together his rich political insights along with the lessons of leadership that flow from the success and failures of several Presidents. This is a must read for all students of leadership."—**Dr. Thomas Saporito, Chairman, RHR International**

"Drawing important lessons from US Presidents, Dennis Powell imparts his exceptional strategic know-how in Leading From the Top. *Essential reading for those in business, nonprofits, politics, and government —and those who enjoy watching the game. Buy this book— now!"*—**Nancy Moses, Chair PA Historical and Museum Commission, author Fakes, Forgeries, and Frauds & Stolen, Smuggled, and Sold: On the Hunt for Cultural Treasures**

"Dennis uses some of the most consequential issues in history to demonstrate what to do, why to do it and, critically, what not to do. A creative way of identifying some very important lessons for leaders and communicators." —**Thomas Gailey, President, GaileyMurray Communications**

"Too often, we don't learn from history and repeat mistakes. What I love about this book is the refresh it provides about how former U.S. presidents navigated crisis, the intricacies most people don't fully grasp, and the parallels we can glean from them."—**Natalie Pantaleo, Marketing-Communications Consultant, www.TheInsideOutMarketer.com, and Author of Lying Down with Dogs**

Foreword

Issues come in all shapes and sizes. Some are minor, and others can bring an organization to a standstill and threaten its sustainability. Issues management is the process of creating solutions and covers everything from framing the problem correctly to managing a crisis. To be successful requires leadership, focus, strategy, and a resolute commitment to the process.

Bernard Baruch, investor and statesman, said: "Whatever failures I have known, whatever errors I have committed, whatever follies I have witnessed in public and private life, have been the consequences of action without thought." This statement captures that essence of issues management: assessment precedes action because activity is no substitute for strategy.

John Foster Dulles said: "The measure of success is not whether you have a tough problem to deal with, but whether it is the same problem you had last year." Failing to frame the right problem is a fundamental error in issues management. It is much like diagnosing and treating the wrong illness because you jumped to a conclusion after assessing early symptoms.

Management consultant Peter Drucker amplifies this point writing: "The most serious mistakes are not being made as a result of wrong answers. The truly dangerous thing is asking the wrong questions." The willingness to question everything, including long-held beliefs and business practices, is essential in the process.

Successful issues management is also inexorably linked to quality leadership. General Douglas MacArthur said: "A true leader has the confidence to stand alone, the courage to make tough decisions, and the compassion to listen to the needs of others." Leaders make the tough calls as events are unfolding. They are not only expected to make the right calls but also to accept responsibility for mistakes. Great leaders are in tune with the environment in which they operate. They listen, encourage constructive feedback, and keep their team informed and engaged. Several of the presidents we examine in this book isolated themselves from constructive feedback and paid dearly.

Another key to successful issues management is planning. Winston Churchill said: "Those who plan do better than those who do not plan, even though they rarely stick to their plan." Plans orchestrate issues management. Without one, an effort can quickly become cacophonous. The plan is the roadmap that targets a destination and provides direction about how to get there. It is very hard to create momentum without a plan.

Benjamin Franklin said: "You may delay, but time will not." This is another key to successful issues management—tie goals to deadlines. A common mistake made by a leader is demanding perfection before advancing to the next step. Delay can derail a plan, so knowing when to move on, even when only limited success is achieved, is key.

Many books have been written about issues management. Several bestsellers are case studies that highlight successes and failures or "how to" books that focus on the process. The experts who wrote these books provide valuable lessons and insights about organizations managing issues and are worth reading.

This book takes a slightly different approach. It spans 15 presidents over nearly a century, 1932 through 2023, who faced a broad range of issues and assesses one issue each managed. In each chapter, lessons are provided based on an assessment of each president as an issues manager. The book covers successes and failures and focuses on the president's issues management skills rather than the politics of issues.

The reason for using presidents to teach lessons in issues management is that readers are familiar with their presidencies and with many of the issues they managed. What is new is that these issues are in an easy to understand format, so they can be quickly recalled and applied to issues you may face.

What is an example of a lesson you can learn from reading this book? A lot has changed between the election of Franklin D. Roosevelt in 1932 to manage the Great Depression and the election of Joe Biden in 2020 to manage Covid-19, but the principles of issues management have remained largely intact and are as fresh today as they were in the context in which both are assessed. FDR asked for permission from the voters to transform the relationship between the American people and the federal government, and he was given a "blank check" to carry out his plan. President Biden largely pursued transformation without permission during his first year in office, and his approval ratings suffered as a result. Permission is a very simple lesson in issues management, but when examined within the context of two presidencies, we see its importance.

The managing of issues by presidents also provides lessons that are applicable in helping the leader of an organization avoid some of the pitfalls that even the most powerful men on earth faced, as well as rules to help in the successful management of issues. In the words of author Edwin Louis Cole: "You don't drown by falling in the water; you drown by staying there." One of the greatest failures in issues management is failing to act, and one of the greatest shortcomings is failing to respond strategically when managing a complex issue. The objective is to not allow an issue to grow into a crisis and a crisis to become unmanageable. There are examples in this book of presidents who made these common mistakes.

A good issues manager has the ability to focus and merge resources into a plan to achieve a successful outcome. This requires a linear approach to problem-solving wherein you are headed in a defined direction toward a solution. The opposite is the circular approach. This is when an issue is poorly framed and the real problem is not identified. When managing this way, whether you start clockwise or counterclockwise, you will end up where you started. The first rule of successful issues management is to flatten the issue.

If, as a reader, one lesson contained in this book helps you to avoid an issue becoming a crisis by employing issues management best practices, then the book's purpose will have been realized.

CHAPTER 1

Issues Management Overview

In any moment of decision, the best thing you can do is the right thing, the next best thing is the wrong thing, and the worst thing you can do is nothing.

—President Theodore Roosevelt

Issues management is practiced at the intersection of business and politics. Many of the skills that serve you well as a business leader are challenged in different ways when managing an issue that may require you to address external or political concerns. The book looks at issues managed by presidents because they served as chief executives, who today are responsible for an estimated four million employees and a multitrillion-dollar budget. Yet, their power, influence, decision-making, judgment, and character were all challenged by the issues they faced. Some were successful, and others failed. The lessons we present are not limited to a specific time in history or circumstance but rather are relevant and applicable to many situations you face as a leader managing an issue today.

Issues management is a disciplined strategic approach to problem-solving implemented using aligned resources and tactical agility. Issues management requires high level management, leadership, and communications skills. Depending on the issue, it can simultaneously also require resources to be applied internally, externally, and politically. Time is not your friend in issues management. Decision-making usually happens in a compressed period. Therefore, it is important that the leader has a firm grasp on the entire playing field and can adapt to changes in real time.

Issues often evolve as they are being managed as does the environment in which they are managed. An ill-conceived strategy or poor implementation of the plan can thrust an issue quickly into uncharted territory.

Failure to recognize a change in the environment early and adjust to it is one of the primary reasons that problems grow into crises.

There are seven elements to successful issues management all of which are required:

1. **Understanding the Problem**: Albert Einstein allegedly said, "If I had an hour to solve a problem, I would spend fifty-five minutes understanding the problem and five minutes on the solution." Very often not enough time is spent on understanding and framing the right problem when managing an issue. The main causes are the pressure to deliver results quickly and lack of objectivity—confirmation bias—about an issue that hits too close to home.

2. **Developing a Strategy**: Strategy is the plan that moves you from where you are to where you need to go. Strategy provides the framework or roadmap for how the issue will be brought to an acceptable conclusion. Strategy defines how resources will be used; the team that will implement the plan of action and the financial resources it will take to accomplish clearly stated goals and benchmarks for success. A common mistake is not having a strategy in place before you make your first move. This creates an environment in which you are reacting rather than managing the issue to your benefit. In short, you will be playing catch-up right out of the gate.

3. **Setting Goals**: Defining what success looks like at the beginning cannot be overstated. Often in issues management the "red light" flashing to warn that you have gone as far as you can is ignored because the end point has not been clearly defined. Defining success requires a realistic assessment of each goal you have set. Note, not all issues management ends in achieving a clear victory or a complete solution. Goals may have to be more nuanced and limited in scope, like turning down the "heat" being generated by the issue rather than eliminating it. The key is to keep goals on top of mind throughout the process so that you are clear on when to stop executing your plan. Failure to do so will create a whole new set of issues.

4. **Aligning Resources**: Issues management will expose any operational weakness within your organizational structure and exploit it. This is why a full and honest assessment of your internal capabilities is

required as part of your planning process. You may not need robust strategic communications daily, but when facing an external or political challenge you likely will need to bolster communications. The caution here is don't hire consultants without a good rationale. "Panic Hires" can deplete resources quickly before the issue is brought to a successful conclusion.

5. **Making the Right First Move**: As much time as possible should be spent making sure that the first move you make is the right move. The initial action will create momentum for what is to follow and allow the leader to properly sequence subsequent actions to maintain and build on it. The first move should advance strategy, clearly establish direction, and help gain control of the narrative. The wrong first move is usually a result of a poorly framed issue or wanting results too quickly.

6. **Achieving Tactical Agility**: Adjusting to change is the norm in issues management. The better able you are to quickly respond to changes that threaten to derail your strategy, the more effective you will be at issues management. There will always be brushfires to put out, and no plan is perfect from the outset. The "fog of war" is very real in issues management when things start to change at many levels simultaneously. General Dwight Eisenhower said: "In preparing for battle I have always found that plans are useless, but planning is indispensable." Establishing clear goals and doing in-depth assessments of resources and capabilities before implementing the plan will optimally position an organization for success.

7. **Gathering Intelligence**: Issues management plans are not cooking or baking recipes. Leaders need to continually measure the results being achieved and adjust the plan as needed. Achieving the desired result is rarely a straight line to the goal. A good rule to follow is "action-assessment-action." This will help you avoid continuing a course of action too long and not getting the desired results leading to lost time and squandered resources.

As a college course, issues management would be taught as part of a leadership, management, communications, and public-relations curriculum because it uses components of each. It also incorporates elements of history and political science. Although every issue has its unique qualities, there are markers that can help the leader avoid making common mistakes. Several of these markers will be presented in context as the actions of the 15 presidents outlined in this book are assessed. I want to stress that the list of lessons presented in each chapter is by no means exhaustive. In fact, I encourage readers to question and reinterpret the lessons advanced.

An issues management leader should possess the following 10 qualities, but where qualities are absent or not sufficiently developed, the leader should bring onto the team or hire an external resource to fill this need.

Strategist—Demonstrable skills to incorporate assets into a well thought-out and executable plan of action to reach well-defined goals.

Issue Framer—Ability to see a problem clearly and articulate its cause concisely.

Goal Setter—Realistic in matching goals with resources and capabilities in order to create the right balance in order to succeed.

Planner—Highly developed time management skills and ability to adapt to change in real time.

Communicator—Making the complex understandable and tasks executable to maintain consistency in plan implementation and control of the narrative.

Engagement—Effective outreach to diverse groups of stakeholders and constituencies in order secure buy-in and maintain support.

Consensus Builder—Skill at bringing diverse viewpoints and needs to coalesce around a single plan of action.

Evaluator—Realistic in assessing and aligning the resources needed to implement the plan of action effectively and efficiently.

Tactician—Demonstrated ability to quickly discern when a change in course is required.

Achiever—The corollary to goal setting is achieving progress in a timely and cost-effective manner.

Peter Drucker wrote: "Management is doing things right; Leadership is doing the right things." This is an important lesson in issues management because you do not want to win the battle while sowing the seeds for new problems to be created by your plan of action. A firm rule is that success in issues management is directly correlated to the quality of leadership within an organization, and great leaders do the right things because they possess good instincts and sound judgment. These qualities will often tip the scale in your favor to achieve better outcomes.

Issues management is by its nature disruptive. Success very much hinges on leaders who effectively identify and manage their weakest links because they know that strategy implementation will fail at the weakest part of the organization. This process demands the best from leaders without whom the worst of an organization will be exposed.

President John F. Kennedy said: "When written in Chinese, the word 'crisis' is composed of two characters. One represents danger and the other represents opportunity." Issues management always brings with it change. Anticipating, assessing, and using change to your benefit can provide significant benefits to your organization. Resisting or not recognizing that change is needed can put your strategy and organization at risk.

The issues the selected presidents managed in the following chapters revealed their true strengths and weaknesses each possessed. It is required that issues managers do not blame others or dodge accountability. Also, every member of your team must take responsibility for the success or failure of the portion of the plan that is their responsibility. Within the issues management process, the best will rise to the top and the weaknesses of others on the team will be exposed. Some members of your team will exceed your expectations and others will fall short. In the end you will know who you can count on going forward.

Former heavyweight champion "Iron" Mike Tyson said: "Everyone has a plan until they get punched in the mouth." Under extreme pressure, things change rapidly and having prepared for every eventuality in advance improves your ability to respond correctly even when managing a moving target. Many organizations begin the issues management process with the belief that they have a great team, but that can all change once the process begins.

The key to all successful issues management is leadership. "Leadership is a potent combination of strategy and character. But if you must be without one, be without the strategy," said General Norman Schwarzkopf, who was the commander in the First Persian Gulf War. Some issues managers are chosen because of their demonstrated abilities and others are trained. The one constant in leadership is the strength of character. True leaders inspire others. They make the weak strong and allow those they lead to exceed any self-imposed limitations.

Former president Ronald Reagan said: "The greatest leader is not necessarily the one who does the greatest things. He is the one that gets people to do the greatest things." Usually, the best plans are implemented by a team rather than one person. Having great lieutenants is a tremendous asset in issues management. Several of the presidents, often retreated within themselves when faced with a crisis and did not seek the counsel of others. This created an environment in which failure was far more likely to be the result. As a leader you are not expected to do everything well. Be willing to lean on others when needed.

General George S. Patton said: "Don't tell people how to do things; tell them what to do and let them surprise you with their results." This strikes a good balance between freedom and control. Micromanagement often backfires because it impedes people who are ready and able to take the initiative when the moment demands it. Each member of the team should understand the broad objectives you are trying to reach and act accordingly. Let your team surprise you with the results they attain through their own initiative. In the best-case scenario, everyone operates from the same playbook, and each member of the team contributes their special talents toward attaining the stated goals. How this happens in issues management, similar to the ways it happens on the battlefield, is often unplanned.

Rev. Dr. Martin Luther King Jr. added this about leadership: "A genuine leader is not a searcher for consensus but a molder of consensus." One of the most important jobs for the leader is to formulate the strategy and then make sure that everyone understands and buys into it. The worst thing to have is members of your team who doubt the efficacy of the strategy you are executing. President George H.W. Bush would recruit a coalition of nations numbering nearly 50 to join in purpose to oust Saddam Hussein's army from Kuwait. President Bush took a "one-team with one-goal approach" to waging war. The goal was clearly and simply stated. Everyone understood the mission. When the goal was achieved, the hostilities ceased, even though there were other military opportunities available to the forces on the ground. Defining success, and building consensus around it, are critical to successful issues management.

"Progress occurs when courageous, skillful leaders seize the opportunity to change things for the better" are the words of former president Harry S. Truman. Again, change is a natural outcome of issues management. New opportunities are usually positive for an organization when managed effectively. It is the role of an effective issues management leader to recognize and seize an opportunity and skillfully frame it, sell it internally, and develop and execute a plan to pursue it to the organization's advantage. This requires a proactive approach. Early in the book, President Truman will be faced with the great challenge of whether to drop the atomic bomb on Japanese civilians or invade Japan. There was no easy choice; only two bad alternatives, but a decision had to be made. He would choose to bring the war to an end quickly. This would require killing 80,000 Japanese civilians in 10 minutes. At the time, under those conditions, it was the right choice as measured by public acceptance.

Former general Colin Powell focused on trust: "The day soldiers stop bringing you their problems is the day you have stopped leading them." To be effective at issues management you need to be willing to listen. Key people need to trust you enough to bring you problems that may not always put them in the best light. It is important for a leader to deftly create a culture where everyone understands that optimal performance is the focus and that problems dilute this focus and can harm strategy implementation. The leader needs to highly value and reward early problem identification and convey this to the team.

Former British prime minister Tony Blair focused on the importance of the term "no" in managing issues: "The art of leadership is saying no, not yes. It is very easy to say yes." The role of the leader is to make decisions about what actions are green-lighted to go forward and what actions need to be delayed or eliminated. Everyone wants to contribute to the effort, but this can result in "strategy contamination," where an organization has multiple activities happening at the same time resulting in slowing the attainment of primary goals. This is why it is so important to state goals clearly and define success unambiguously. When success is achieved, have the good sense to stop solving the problem, no matter how many new opportunities the crisis has created. This is the most important and consequential "no" a leader will need to say.

In the end, there are only four outcomes that can be achieved when managing issues:

- **Win-Win**: The issue is brought to a successful conclusion—goal achieved—without any detrimental fallout to the organization.
- **Win-Lose**: This is when an issue is brought to a somewhat favorable conclusion, but within the process of managing it, seeds are sown for other issues to develop in the future. This is usually a result of poor framing of the issue, eagerness to show results too quickly, skipping important steps in the process, rigidly holding on to failed strategy, not recognizing personal biases, insufficient intelligence gathering, or failure to fully understand the changing nature of the issue you are solving.
- **Lose-Win**: This is when only part of a bigger issue is resolved in the short term, but the partial solution creates the environment where the remaining issues can be more effectively managed going forward. This is a positive outcome where the leader is very clear about what is possible at the time with the resources available.
- **Lose-Lose**: This is when the strategy fails, the issue is not resolved, and support, confidence, and goodwill are all diminished while carrying out your plan. There is usually little left to salvage from a "lose-lose" outcome for the current leadership, and the next in line is often tasked with cleaning up the mess. This is usually a result of poor framing of the issue, making the wrong first move, failure to sufficiently align operationally, being late to the game in managing an issue that has become a crisis, and failing to choose the right leader.

The focus of this book is to help you to better understand issues management by looking at the 15 people who managed the most complex issues, on the biggest stage, under the constant scrutiny of the media and the public.

We will look at one key issue faced by each president, from Franklin Roosevelt to Donald J. Trump, and examine what they did right, what mistakes they made, and what we can learn from each of them. Lastly, the Biden presidency will be assessed not by issues managed poorly, but by showing issues that were allowed to grow into crises by being ignored. The book will end by summarizing lessons learned in a broader context to serve as a summary.

Analyzing presidents provides a foundation built on common understandings. We have all studied history and most who read this book will have some level of awareness and understanding of the events surrounding each of the 15 issues in focus.

The lessons gleaned from each president's actions will not necessarily directly parallel the points made in this chapter. Rather, it is my hope that they will serve to amplify them by adding additional context and meaning to each item on the list. It is also my hope that senior managers will find these lessons useful and applicable in problem-solving, issues management, strategic communications, crisis management, and stakeholder engagement going forward.

Each chapter provides background to supply the reader with context. It then lays out lessons that can be learned from how the issue was managed. It will then provide an analysis of the decision or event focused on issues management best practices. The lessons, hopefully, will be interesting as well as educational and aid in your decision-making, planning, and successful issues management going forward.

CHAPTER 2

Roosevelt—Asking Permission

We begin our study of presidents as issues managers with Franklin D. Roosevelt. As president, he faced two of the major issues of the 20th century—Great Depression and World War II. He was elected president four times which is the most in history. By most accounts he was highly successful as president. As an issues manager the foundation for his success started with a very simple proposition of asking permission from stakeholders.

There is a saying, "I would rather ask forgiveness than permission." The opposite is true in issues management. Securing a mandate for action from key stakeholders is imperative when a solution requires the leader to make major changes. Permission puts the wind at your back and in most cases provides the leader with more latitude to act. As you will read, Roosevelt asked for permission to fundamentally change the relationship between the people and the federal government, and his request was granted by being elected. Had he not asked for permission, the bold actions he took would likely have been slowed or been derailed putting his "New Deal" agenda in peril.

Franklin D. Roosevelt inherited a crisis when he was elected president in 1932, "By 1933, when the Great Depression reached its lowest point ... nearly half the country's banks had failed." The Bureau of Labor Statistics later estimated that "12,830,000 persons were out of work in 1933, about one-fourth of a civilian labor force of over fifty-one million." Roosevelt's campaign, highlighted:

> Hunger stalked the nation and food lines proliferated in major cities. The homeless set up encampments wherever they could, including in Manhattan's Central Park, and they became known

as "Hoovervilles." Private charitable organizations ran out of funds to provide such basic necessities as food, clothing, and medicine.

Roosevelt's analysis of the challenge he faced was a new response that was welcomed by the voters.

In a groundbreaking speech in September 1932 at the Commonwealth Club in San Francisco, candidate Roosevelt challenged existing beliefs about the role of government in society. He argued it should be expanded to include "distributing wealth and products more equitably, adapting existing economic organizations to the service of the people," and he proclaimed: "Every man has a right to life; and this means that he also has a right to make a comfortable living." Roosevelt had positioned himself as a bold problem-solver who was willing to draw outside of the existing lines to find answers. The people responded. On Election Day, Roosevelt carried 42 of the then 48 states and swept Democrats into power in Congress with a mandate for dramatic change.

One lesson is that when something is not working, fix it, and when what you have been doing for a long time does not work anymore, change it. Roosevelt grasped that America was facing not only an economic depression but also a hopeless spirit that was calling out for someone to acknowledge their pain and do something to make it stop.

On March 4, 1933, Franklin Delano Roosevelt delivered his First Inaugural Address in which he clearly stated his mission as president and defined himself as an issues manager:

1. **Framing the Issue**: "So, first of all, let me assert my firm belief that the only thing we have to fear is fear itself … In every dark hour of our national life, a leadership of frankness and vigor has met with the understanding and support of the people themselves, which is essential to victory. I am convinced that you will again give that support to leadership in these critical days."

2. **Defining the Problem**: "Plenty is at our doorstep, but a generous use of it languishes in the very sight of the supply. Primarily, this is because the rulers of the exchange of mankind's goods have failed … Practices of the unscrupulous money changers stand indicted in the court of public opinion, rejected by the hearts and minds of men."

3. **Articulating the Rationale**: "Restoration calls, however, not for changes in ethics alone. This nation asks for action, and action is needed now. Our greatest primary task is to put people to work. This is not an unsolvable problem if we face it wisely and courageously. It can be accomplished in part by direct recruiting by the Government itself, treating the task as we would treat the emergency of a war, but at the same time, through this employment, accomplishing greatly needed projects to stimulate and reorganize the use of our natural resources."

4. **Affirming his Mandate**: "I am prepared under my constitutional duty to recommend the measures that a stricken nation in the midst of a stricken world may require. These measures, or such other measures as the Congress may build out of its experience and wisdom, I shall seek, within my constitutional authority, to bring to speedy adoption."

5. **Defining the Path**: "We do not distrust the future of essential democracy. The people of the United States have not failed. In their need, they have registered a mandate that they want direct, vigorous action. They have asked for discipline and direction under leadership. They have made me the present instrument of their wishes. In the spirit of the gift, I take it."

His action was swift and decisive. On March 5, 1933, the day after he was sworn in as president, Roosevelt declared a "Bank Holiday," where he ordered the closing of banks for several days to stop the runs on deposits that were leading banks to fail. Four days later, he signed into law the Emergency Banking Relief Act, which created government bank examiners who would go to banks to assess their financial health. These actions were important because they produced results quickly. Note that quick results are best practice only when they advance overall strategy. Action for the sake of action is a bad issues management practice.

In his first Fireside Chat with the American people on radio, Roosevelt provided context for government action by saying, "Your Government does not intend that the history of the past few years shall be repeated. We do not want and will not have another epidemic of bank failures." Roosevelt knew that one action would not end the Great Depression, but he also recognized that keeping his stakeholders informed and engaged would maintain support at a high level. Roosevelt used radio to control the narrative. The number of people tuning in to listen would exceed 61,000,000 during his terms as president.

Roosevelt understood that spending as his only tool could open the door for critics, so he created new revenue streams. On March 22, 1933, Roosevelt signed into law the Beer and Wine Revenue Act, which would be the precursor to the repeal of prohibition in America. Briefly, "This law levies a federal tax on all alcoholic beverages to raise revenue for the federal government and gives individual states the option to further regulate the sale and distribution of beer and wine."

He also incorporated into his plan ways to expand his base of support. In May 1933, Roosevelt signed the Federal Emergency Relief Administration (FERA). It provided direct cash relief to citizens through a program wherein the federal government provided money to the states, which distributed the funds to the people in the form of grants. Also, "One of the most significant FERA policies was to grant relief without discrimination. Blacks, especially in the South, who had never gotten anything from the government, suddenly found themselves eligible for federal relief." Roosevelt's skillful issues management to attract new support and voters to his cause, created the modern Democratic coalition of voters.

He did not stop there. Roosevelt changed the relationship between the federal government and farmers through the Agricultural Adjustment Act and Farm Credit Act; energy producers with the creation of the Tennessee Valley Authority; conservationists by expanding the scope of the National Parks Service; home buyers by entering the home loan business with the Home Owners' Loan Act; banks with the passage of the Federal Deposit Insurance Corporation; constructors through the Public Works Administration; and artists through the Public Works of Art Project. His strategy fundamentally transformed the relationship between the states and the federal government and between the people and the federal government.

There are two other big lessons to learn from Roosevelt's actions early in the "New Deal." The first is you must produce results. Decisive actions and popular programs mean little if there is no change in the trajectory of the crisis. Roosevelt was able to deliver results from his early response. During

1933, "Unemployment dropped from 22.9 percent to 20.6 percent," and indices across the board improved A seminal point in issues management is when the bleeding stops, the healing begins. In other words, when things begin to move in a more positive direction, support grows, and the stakeholders want more.

There is a note of caution here. The bigger the crisis, the more room the leader has to implement dramatic change once he has secured the trust of the stakeholders. The problem is that you can get lost in crisis management and be lured into believing that you must produce something new all the time to keep your momentum going. A rule of issues management is to define success at the beginning and when you have achieved it STOP implementing the plan.

There often comes a point in issues management when the leader needs to assess who are friends and who are foes. In January 1934, Roosevelt delivered his first State of the Union Address to Congress, where he would draw his line in the sand:

> Now that we are definitely in the process of recovery lines have been rightly drawn between those to whom this recovery means a return to old methods—and the number of these people is small—and those for whom recovery means a reform of many old methods, a permanent readjustment of many of our ways of thinking, and therefore of many of our social and economic arrangements.

Roosevelt pulled no punches: "The money changers have fled from their high seats in the temple of our civilization. We may now restore that temple to the ancient truths." And he provided another call to action, "Restoration calls, however, not for changes in ethics alone. This nation asks for action, and action now."

Roosevelt enjoyed high approval ratings in 1934. Research reported by Vassar College found: "A poll of nearly 1.8 million Americans conducted by The Literary Digest found that 61% approved of President Roosevelt's policies and 39% disapproved." In 1934, Roosevelt won another electoral mandate in the midterm elections, retaining solid majorities in both houses of congress. He was rewarded because he had defined the crisis, deftly assessed its severity, addressed the issues that were driving it, and delivered results.

At the end of 1934, economic data continued to be favorable. The unemployment rate was down to 16 percent; gross domestic product saw a 16.9 percent increase. The Dow Jones stood at 104, up from 60 in 1932, and there were only nine bank failures—compared to 4,000 in 1933. The "New Deal" was a measurable success, so Roosevelt decided we needed more of it. This trend would continue through 1935.

Roosevelt would be rewarded with a resounding victory in his reelection in 1936. In that election, he won more than 96 percent of the electoral votes, defeating Republican Alf Landon. Arthur Krock would chronicle Roosevelt's victory for *The New York Times* writing,

> the President was the choice of a vast preponderance of the voters in all parts of the country, and with him were re-elected as Vice President John N. Garner of Texas and an almost untouched Democratic majority in the House of Representatives.

Roosevelt's mandate was affirmed.

In his Second Inaugural Address, Roosevelt would frame the challenge as, "I see one-third of a nation ill-housed, ill-clad, ill-nourished … The test of our progress is not whether we add more to the abundance of those who have much; it is whether we provide enough for those who have too little." He would go on to say:

> Today we reconsecrate our country to long-cherished ideals in a suddenly changed civilization. In every land there are always at work forces that drive men apart and forces that draw men together. In our personal ambitions we are individualists. But in our seeking for economic and political progress as a nation, we all go up, or else we all go down, as one people.

He was in full control of the narrative, but he was further defining the problem rather than setting and achieving goals. The nature of the problem changes over time. It is important for the issues manager to understand these subtle shifts and adjust to them.

The Franklin Delano Roosevelt (FDR) Library wrote this about the start of his second term:

> Flushed with victory, the emboldened President overreached. A divisive battle with the Supreme Court and an unsuccessful effort to "purge" conservatives from the Democratic Party energized his opponents. Economic setbacks added to his woes. FDR's reform agenda stalled, and events overseas began to take his administration in a vastly different direction.

There can be a degree of arrogance that comes with power. Roosevelt's early successes in managing the Great Depression were aided by passing program after program through a decidedly Democratic Congress. His out with the old and in with the new strategy had begun to look more like out with the new and in with the newer. Roosevelt had gotten the federal government's nose under just about every tent to regulate business, fund new programs, build infrastructure, and provide federal relief directly to individuals. He had ruled supreme. But you reach the point where managing an issue has no clear end point. The economy in 1937 was much stronger than the one he inherited in 1933. His bold playbook had worked, but Roosevelt's decision was to keep sending in more plays.

At the end of 1937, unemployment stood at 9.1 percent. The next year, it rose to 12.5 percent. The Dow index, which stood at 188 in 1936, would slide to 122 in 1937, rise to 154 in 1938, and fall to 150 in 1939. The "New Deal" had stalled.

Roosevelt, the leader, was given a broad mandate to act and he initially acted decisively to improve the American economy. The point when he maybe should have tapped the brakes is not clear, but at some point, he found himself reforming for the sake of reform. This is common in issue management when you are right on point in framing the issue and your initial actions are highly successful. The problem was that Roosevelt had not defined achievable success continuously and he reached a point of diminishing returns.

Lessons

At Issue: President Roosevelt received a mandate by winning an electoral landslide to take decisive action to get America out of the Great Depression.

Lesson: President Roosevelt showed the importance of asking for and being given a permission to act before implementing his strategy.

1. **Accurate Analysis:** Everyone saw the crisis created by the Great Depression, but Roosevelt was quick to figure out that the problem could not be solved by doing what was traditionally done. There was running room to Hoover's left and a lot of it. By filling this void, Roosevelt gave himself an open field where he controlled the narrative because he defined the message. Simply put, the American people accepted that the problem could not be solved without significant levels of government stimulation and action and Roosevelt was not afraid to go down this path.

2. **Clear Choice:** Roosevelt's strategic choice to the American people was, do you want more of the same or a change in course? He knew the answer because he understood the environment in which the choice would be made. He understood his audience. Creating a simple, clear question or choice is where you want to be in issues management in securing permission to act boldly to get results. When you can boil it down to this level of clarity and simplicity, you are usually winning.

3. **Maintained Integrity:** There was no bait and switch with FDR. What he did was what he had promised to do in his campaign. Roosevelt was as advertised and because there were no surprises, Roosevelt was able to keep his base intact and even start to build support beyond those who elected him. A high level of consistency, honesty and transparency are vital to successful issues management. In Roosevelt's case, it allowed him to bring doubters and fence sitters to his side and continue to grow his popularity, which translated into political power.

4. **The Right First Move:** The promise of action brings with it a pledge to get things moving quickly. Roosevelt had to select his first move carefully. It had to be quick, decisive, and most importantly, it had to be doable and deliver results. Roosevelt probably would have met a different fate in terms of improving his popularity and support had he taken on an issue with a longer time horizon right out of the gate. Here

I am talking about six months being too long. By making the "Bank Holiday" his first move, he positioned himself to be green-lighted for more action. By closing the banks and establishing oversight, Roosevelt sent the message to the people that "I have your backs." It was the first step in reestablishing confidence, and as Roosevelt said, "nothing to fear but fear itself." His action helped people believe this was true.

5. **Avoid Third Rail**: Roosevelt was not a revolutionary, but he did radically change the relationship between the federal government and the people. He colored outside the lines but not too far. He understood that there was a third rail on the track that could derail his "New Deal," and that was the American people believing he was a socialist. He prioritized his responses, realizing that the American people would accept reforms to capitalism but were not likely to accept a dramatic shift to socialism. Most issues have a third rail on which your efforts can be redefined in an unfavorable light. In developing your plan of action be mindful of this and build into your plan ways to avoid it, and when you cannot, try to mitigate its negative impacts.

6. **Read the Room**: Although a patrician by station, Roosevelt understood and articulated the fears and frustrations of the American people. When a CEO speaks publicly as part of a crisis team, she is not talking to her Board of Directors or executive team but rather to those who are most directly impacted. A leader needs to deliver a message that connects with her audience at the logical, emotional, and visceral levels. The importance of connecting with your audience cannot be overstated.

7. **Use of Media**: Through his Fireside Chats, Roosevelt connected with the American people and controlled the narrative. He would only do thirty during his 11 plus years in office, but the political benefits were tremendous in maintaining support. The media has changed since Roosevelt, but it still provides the issues manager with the opportunity to connect with the audience and rise above the noise. A comprehensive media plan is part of any good plan of action.

8. **Leveraging Success**: Success opens the door to propose even bolder solutions. Roosevelt's program continued to grow in scope because

it was built on the solid foundation of asking permission and then showing that your plan is producing results Roosevelt's expansion of government was powered by trust. You cannot underestimate the power of trust in issues management.

9. **Build a Great Team**: Roosevelt surrounded himself with capable people, whom he called his "brain trust." They were people able to think creatively and craft nontraditional solutions to problems. In times of crisis, having a great CEO may not be enough. You also need strength at the operational and tactical levels to coordinate resources and implement the plan. Failure to properly staff at all levels can derail your plan quickly.

10. **Comprehensive Approach**: Roosevelt's solutions were broad-based, touching every element of society and aspect of the economy. His knack for inclusion kept his detractors from gaining momentum, which propelled him to his overwhelming electoral victory in 1936. Bringing people under your tent is almost always a good thing when managing an issue, this is why you should never close the door on anyone willing to help and never write off an opponent completely.

11. **Momentum**: Roosevelt never lost focus in the initial stages of the "New Deal;" therefore, he never lost momentum Roosevelt controlled the narrative from the beginning of his campaign in 1932, into the late 1930s, when the economic numbers began to shift not in his favor. When your plan stalls, do everything you can to regain forward progress, because once momentum is lost it is exceedingly difficult to regain.

12. **Test of Time**: Roosevelt built a brand as a man of action coupled with an image of compassion that transcended politics. In the decades that followed there were no calls to undo what he had done. In fact, the opposite was true as future presidents built on his legacy. As an issues manager you want to create a plan that will stand the test of time whenever possible by making your organization stronger and more resilient as a result of your actions.

Roosevelt's accomplishments were on a grand scale. He would be elected four times. He managed the Great Depression and then most of World War II. Almost every historian ranks him as one of the "Top

Three" presidents in history. He was a man of clarity and action, and he deserves the praise he has received.

Roosevelt would die in office in his fourth term. He would leave a crisis for his successor, Harry S. Truman, to solve as he would face a huge decision right out of the gate concerning how to defeat an intractable enemy—Japan.

CHAPTER 3

Truman—All Fame
in Fleeting

Harry S. Truman provides a valuable lesson to all issues management leaders: Circumstances can change quickly, and you need to prepare your next in command to take the helm without losing any momentum. President Truman would be asked to make a monumental decision after assuming office, upon the passing of President Roosevelt, for which he was not prepared.

Robert Half said: "It is easy to make good decisions where there are no bad options." In issues management, the leader will often be asked to choose between two bad options at critical junctures and decide quickly which choice best advances the strategy. This is why it is so important to state goals clearly and have them understood by your entire team.

On April 12, 1945, President Franklin Delano Roosevelt passed away at his "Little White House" in Warm Springs, Georgia. The last battle of the war in Europe ended five days earlier. Hitler was still alive, but German tyranny in Europe was ending. In the Pacific, the invasion of Okinawa had begun several weeks earlier, and the end of the Japanese empire was certain, although fighting in the Pacific theatre would continue for five more months.

Franklin Roosevelt left behind a world still at war, but his framework for peace would precipitate the "Cold War" as framed by Winston Churchill, which would pit western democracies against the Soviet Union and Eastern Bloc of nations in Europe. In some ways, it was a "win-lose" scenario. Nations would be realigned to achieve peace, but starkly divided ideologically in the wake of World War II. Roosevelt also left behind a vice president, Harry S. Truman, whom he kept out of the loop on one big matter—the development of the atomic bomb.

Harry S. Truman was born in Lamar, Missouri and was a successful farmer before serving as captain of field artillery during World War I. Upon his return from war, he worked as a haberdasher, and became involved in Democratic machine politics in Kansas City. He was elected as an administrative judge in 1922 and then U.S. Senator in 1934. His work in the senate included investigating waste and corruption in World War II.

The reason he became Roosevelt's vice president in 1944 was to shore up support from dissident conservatives and quell opponents who were critical of Roosevelt seeking a fourth term as president. When he was nominated, he was eating a sandwich. His acceptance speech was perhaps the shortest in history, *The New York Times* reported it,

> You won't know how very much I appreciate the very great honor which has come to the State of Missouri. It is also a great responsibility which I am perfectly willing to assume. Nine years and five months ago I came to the Senate. I expect to continue the efforts I have made there to help shorten the war and to win peace under the great leader, Franklin D. Roosevelt. I don't know what else I can say, except that I accept this great honor with all humility. I thank you.

Truman had replaced Henry Wallace as Roosevelt's candidate for vice president in 1944. It was Roosevelt's fourth term, and he was focused on winning the war and crafting peace. He was also in deteriorating health. Since 1933, Roosevelt has been the go-to guy, the decision-maker, and the person in charge. He had little time for Truman and was by nature not a delegator. In fact, Roosevelt and Truman only met eight times before his death. Churchill and Stalin knew about "the bomb" but not Truman.

Upon Roosevelt's passing, Truman told reporters the next day, as reported in *The New Yorker* by Jeffrey Frank, "I have the most terribly responsible job any man ever had." He had no idea how "terribly responsible" it would become and how quickly he would have to make a decision that would change the nature of warfare and the world forever.

About two weeks after assuming his presidency, according to Mr. Frank, Secretary of War Henry Stimson told Truman, "I think it is very important that I should have a talk with you as soon as possible on a highly secret matter." The matter was the Manhattan Project, a research operation unbeknownst to Truman. The weapon was so deadly and horrifying that Robert Oppenheimer, one of the scientists who created it, dedicated his life to controlling the destructive power of the weapon.

There is a lesson here for issues management leaders: Keep key people in the loop on the big issues that matter to the overall success of your project. When there is a change in leadership, for whatever reason, the person should never be caught flat-footed by not having sufficient information when a major decision needs to be made. Organizationally, not having seamless continuity can be costly in terms of time and money and can even derail strategy.

Truman was now commander-in-chief overseeing "Operation Iceberg," which was the name given to the invasion of Okinawa that began on Easter Sunday, April 1, 1945. It was the largest amphibious invasion in history with 545,000 U.S. troops involved. The battle lasted 82 days. The Japanese would suffer more than 100,000 casualties, and the allied forces 50,000. It was also one of the bloodiest battles of the Pacific theatre. The battle ended on June 22, 1945. From Okinawa, the allies had direct access to bomb Japan, having achieved total air superiority. The next step was to invade Japan and end the war.

Note that during these 82 days of battle, President Roosevelt died, and President Truman assumed power and learned of the atomic bomb. It was only six weeks after the Battle of Okinawa ended that President Truman gave the order to drop atomic bombs on Hiroshima and Nagasaki.

In issues management, you are not always presented with only good choices, but rather the best choice and the second-best option. In deciding to drop "the bomb," Truman was expected to skillfully prioritize the war strategy and make the best decision. This was not a decision where the president had to engage the American people to persuade or convince them of the righteousness of his action. It was not the type of decision where you take a poll or ask for a show of hands from your cabinet. This was a situation where the president did not ask permission but may have needed to ask for forgiveness if he was wrong about the result he expected—the bomb would end the war quickly. The "lose-lose" scenario was he would drop the bomb and it would strengthen the resolve of the Japanese who would fight on with increased resolve and ferocity. This would necessitate Truman either continue to drop atomic bombs or invade Japan. He had to make a tough decision. The wrong outcome of his decision would force him to make an even more difficult choice. This is a good example of the highest stakes an issues manager can face.

The decision-making environment was not easy for Truman. He lacked the stature and gravitas of Roosevelt and did not have Roosevelt's reservoir of goodwill to draw upon. The lesson here is you are what the title on the door says you are. When the telephone was answered at Truman's office, the caller was greeted with "president's office." The secretary did not say "new president's office" or "former Vice President Truman's office." Truman was president. Whether you have been on the job for 2 weeks or 11 years, you are now the person in charge and you are expected to make the tough calls and get them right.

In July 1945, Japanese propaganda radio threatened Americans who were preparing to invade Japan saying: "The sooner the Americans come, the better ... One hundred million die proudly." It was an ominous threat, but the Japanese had proven to be a different kind of enemy fighting to the last man, refusing to surrender, launching kamikaze attacks on ships, and military leaders committing suicide when all was lost, as happened on Okinawa.

Everyone knew that invading Japan would be costly in terms of the lives lost. The strategy driving "Operation Downfall" was to invade, occupy, and bring about the unconditional surrender of Japan within 18 months of the defeat of Germany. It would require 1,700,000 U.S. troops, according to the plan. This would bring the war into 1946 and beyond, and millions of lives were predicted to be lost.

Truman along with Great Britain and China issued the Potsdam Declaration in July 1945. It called for Japan's unconditional surrender, or the nation would face "annulation." Japan did not accept the call to surrender, even though, it is argued, they knew at the time that there was no path to victory.

The lesson here is when managing an issue, you don't make idle threats or empty promises. Words and deeds need to always be aligned. Don't start what you can't finish and don't say what you don't mean are good rules of the road.

Truman at this point was aware of the destructive force of the atomic bomb. He had to make assumptions about how the American people would respond to such a horrific weapon. Would the American people understand his rationale for killing 80,000 civilians in mere seconds using the most destructive weapon ever used? Americans had accepted losing men on beachheads over the past four years, but would they understand, comprehend, and forgive death on this scale resulting from one action taken by their president.

In making his decision, Truman kept focused on the primary objective which was to use the bomb to bring a quick end to the war. Success would not mean that Truman would be applauded, but failure could turn public opinion against him, leading to the questioning of his judgment and ability to lead. There was no clear right or wrong choice but rather a better or worse choice when all factors were considered.

Truman acted. As chronicled by the Truman Library,

At 8:15 AM Hiroshima time, "Little Boy" was dropped. The result was approximately 80,000 deaths in just the first few minutes. Thousands died later from radiation sickness. On August 9, 1945, another bomber was enroute to Japan, only this time it was heading for Nagasaki with "Fat Man," another atomic bomb. After the first minute of dropping "Fat Man," 39,000 men, women and children were killed. 25,000 more were injured. Both cities were leveled by the bombs and this, in turn, forced Japan to surrender to the United States. The war was finally over.

His assumptions were correct. In issues management there are often no clear answers to what is the right next move. You must go with your gut based on your experience and the counsel of others.

Truman's rationale, as reported in *The New York Times* upon announcement of the atomic bomb being dropped, was:

It was to spare the Japanese people from utter destruction that the ultimatum of July 26, was issued at Potsdam. Their leaders promptly rejected that ultimatum. If they do not now accept our terms, they may expect a rain of ruin from the air the like of which has never been seen on this earth.

Paul Tibbets, who piloted the Enola Gay, the B-29 from which the bomb over Hiroshima was dropped, summed up the attitudes of many about the event:

> I thought to myself, Gee, if we can be successful, we're going to prove to the Japanese the futility in continuing to fight because we can use those weapons on them. They're not going to stand up to this thing. After I saw what I saw I was more convinced that they're gonna (sic) quit. That's the only way I could do it.

After the war ended, the debate on nuclear weapons would be reframed. The American people were polled about whether nuclear weapons should be under the control of the newly formed United Nations. Most Americans were ambivalent about atomic weapons, wanting to move on with their lives. Issues management is played out in real time. The issue is what it is at that time and place. The dropping of an atomic bomb was the best choice at that time in history, but since 1945 a nuclear bomb has never been dropped on noncombatants in war.

One more lesson is that even the toughest of decisions have a relatively short shelf life. The reality was that the public expected that their president would do whatever was necessary to end the war. The people were thankful, but soon moved on to other things and made new demands on their president.

During his presidency, Truman would be the first president to focus on stopping the expansion of communism. The Truman Doctrine focused on keeping communism out of Greece and Turkey. He would spearhead the rebuilding of Europe with the Marshall Plan. In response to a Soviet blockade of Berlin in 1948, Truman ordered the Berlin Airlift. He supported international organizations and alliances, including the United Nations and North Atlantic Treaty Organization (NATO). He signed into law the National Security Act which created the Central Intelligence Agency. He began the process to desegregate the armed forces of the United States. He opened the door to 200,000 European immigrants displaced by war. And, he involved us in conflict in Korea and ushered in the era of the Cold War.

Truman would narrowly win the presidency in 1948. This was only a little more than three years after he made the decision to drop the bomb and end the war.

By 1948, the glow of victory had dulled. People moved on. Priorities changed. There were now deep divisions that had developed within the Democratic Party. The "Dixiecrats" were southern Democrats who wanted greater emphasis on states' rights within the party. Truman supported civil rights. There was also a wing of the party that was isolationist and wanted to retreat from foreign affairs. This group, led by Henry Wallace, former vice president under Roosevelt, fractured into a progressive faction. Truman's policies were tough on Russia and urged engagement in the world. He believed this was the best policy for the nation in the postwar world. By 1952, a seemingly unwinnable war in Korea, firing of hero General Douglas MacArthur, accusations of corruption, inflation, and an economy struggling to regain its footing postwar, dropped Truman's support to a record low in the polls. The public would vote to turn the page in 1952.

Lessons

At Issue: President Truman needed to decide about whether to drop atomic bombs on the citizens of Japan or invade the Japanese mainland at the cost of millions of lives.

Lesson: There are times when you need to choose between the better of two bad options and the decision is yours alone to make.

1. **Ownership**: The decision to drop the bomb was Truman's decision alone. He could not use the goodwill or the memory of Franklin Roosevelt, who had developed the weapon, to justify his decision or mitigate any fallout from failure to achieve his stated goal. Truman was in charge, and the American people expected him to act like he was in charge. The issues management leader cannot claim that the problem did not develop on my watch, therefore, you must blame the other guy. If an issue is being managed on your watch, then you own it.

2. **Positioning**: As president, Truman was chief executive, commander-in-chief, and leader of the Democratic Party. He skillfully positioned the issue as a wartime decision which removed it from politics and distanced it from policy. There are different standards applied in a time of war when destruction and death are givens. The decision was made with Truman acting in his capacity as leader of our military. As an issues manager you hold a position within an organization, but you are also a member of the community and part of a family. In issues management, context serves to frame issues, and actions flow from this framing.

3. **Goal**: Dropping the bomb had one objective: Bringing a terrible war to an end quickly and saving lives. Truman was not asserting a policy that stated we would use the weapon to bend the world to our will. This would have gone beyond his mandate to act. In issues management, you are often faced with a tough choice of how to use power to solve a problem. It is wise to use power sparingly and to clearly distinguish that what you do in crisis is not your policy going forward.

4. **Rationale**: The American people wanted peace and achieving that outcome faster and at the cost of fewer American lives was a "win-win" in the eyes of the American people in 1945. Truman was in step with public opinion in making his decision to drop the bomb. It is always best when your rationale for action comports with the public's view of the wise of just decision.

5. **Data**: Data must have context and be overlaid with strategy to advance an issue. Truman had two data sets to use to make his case and position his decision. The first was the substantial number of lives that would be lost in an invasion of Japan. The second the terror unleased by the bomb would speed up surrender. Information in issues management can be your best friend or worst enemy. It must be used correctly in making the case for action.

6. **Building Credibility**: Truman got the result he wanted. Japan announced its surrender on August 15, 1945. This is less than a week after the bombing of Nagasaki. Having your assumptions play out is always a good thing when managing an issue. When you are right you are rewarded with enhanced credibility and usually given more leeway for your next moves. It is important not to guess when

managing an issue, provide false hope or mislead. If you say something will be completed the next day, then make sure it is because
your credibility is at stake.

7. **The Bigger Issues**: The American people would celebrate the end
of the war rather than focus on the unleashing of the nuclear age in
warfare. This meant they would not dwell on Truman's decision and
would quickly move on to other matters. Using a nuclear weapon
was the big issue of the moment, but it was trumped by the desire
of the public to move on from the war. As an issues manager, always
try to discern the bigger issues the public will move onto after the
problem has been solved.

8. **Aftermath**: In a poll taken in 1945, after the bombs were dropped,
85 percent of the American people agreed with Truman's action and
the result it produced. It is important to measure the results to confirm success and assess failure. This will help adjust your strategy
and focus your future communications. Remember, the public is
dynamic, and things will change often faster than you would like
them to change.

9. **Branding the Opposition**: Japan was not a sympathetic enemy.
This played to Truman's advantage as our propaganda painted the
Japanese as merciless killers in war. Therefore, selling the idea that
Japan would never surrender was not a heavy lift for Truman. Japan
and the Japanese culture were foreign to most Americans; therefore,
the opportunity existed to brand them in the most negative way.
Branding your opposition to your benefit is often a good tactic to
gain the advantage and create more space in which to operate, especially when you start playing hard ball.

10. **Tragic Necessity**: People understand the reason that in medical
emergencies, doctors perform triage to save those on the margin
between life and death while not attending to those who are likely
lost and those who will likely survive. In warfare people accept killing as necessary and just to protect their interests. When faced with
two bad choices, people understand that you must decide and will
support the lesser of two evils as the better choice.

11. **Moving On**: Truman was not paralyzed by what would happen
down the road after he made his decision. Decisions are made to

address the problem at hand. Whatever happens after that will be dealt with at the appropriate time. You should not replay a decision over and over in your head asking "what if" questions. You did your best. Move on.

12. **All Fame Is Fleeting**: There are no curtain calls in issues management. Truman was not placed on a pedestal for ending World War II with one bold move. It did not win him the undying loyalty of the American people. New issues would change the political environment as loyalties shifted over time. What is important is that you learn from each issue you manage and use this knowledge to improve your capabilities, build your brand and promote your interests.

Winston Churchill said: "Success is not final, failure is not fatal: it is the courage to continue that counts."

Next up, we look at the general who led allied forces to victory in Europe who will face the issue of racial justice in public education.

CHAPTER 4

Eisenhower—Making an Issue Manageable

Warren Buffet frames this chapter very well: "In looking for people to hire, you look for three qualities: integrity, intelligence, and energy. And if they do not have the first, the other two will kill you." In issues management integrity counts. This may mean doing things that do not expedite the solution because they are the right things to do. Dwight Eisenhower provides a master class in issues management during a time of fundamental social change in America.

In selecting Eisenhower in 1952, Republicans nominated a true American hero. War veterans were becoming the dominant generation in America. "Ike," as he was called, would win 442 electoral votes, and carry 39 or the 48 states. The Senate and House were organized by Republicans with narrow majorities in 1953.

On June 25, 1950, the Korean War began under Truman. It was the first war where two nuclear powers were involved. Russia had developed its bomb in 1949. It was also the first time that western nations fought to stop the spread of communism. In the beginning, the conflict was perceived as a good war because the public frame of reference was World War II, where the goal was to take territory and drive your enemy back until it had no room to fight. That was not how the Korean War played out. North Korea was backed by Russia (USSR) and China (PRC), which had become a communist nation in 1949. South Korea was supported by the United Nations backed by the United States. With both sides having access to partners with nuclear weapons, the war would become a stalemate because neither side was able to use its full arsenal of weapons to defeat the other side. Korea was a brutal conflict.

Early in the conflict, Gallup polling reported:

When Americans were first asked, in August 1950, if deciding to defend South Korea was a mistake, only 20% thought it was, while 65% said it was not a mistake. By the following January, opinion had shifted dramatically, and 49% thought the decision was a mistake, while 38% said it was not, and 13% had no opinion.

The growing unpopularity of the war was based on the belief that it was unwinnable and being fought in half measures. Also, Truman's decision to remove World War II hero, General Douglas MacArthur, from command was widely questioned. According to Gallup: "Mr. Truman's popularity, (fell) from an 87 percent approval rating in July 1945 to a 23 percent rating in December 1951."

Truman did not prepare the American people for the savagery of the Korean War or for the complexities of fighting a proxy war which is a war fought by one nation to advance the strategic goals of another nation. There was also the wide acceptance of the "domino effect" that posited that were South Korea to fall next in line was Japan and then communist domination of Asia.

Republicans recruited a proven winner of wars in Eisenhower, and by July 1953, in his first year in office, the fighting war in Korea was over for the United States. A cease-fire divided the nation at the 38th parallel. The American people were not prepared to accept a war that could not be won and were not willing to use the atomic bomb to bend other nations to our will.

In an April of 1953 poll, 69 percent agreed that America should sign an armistice and end the conflict in Korea. In 8 of the past 12 years, the United States had been involved in armed conflict. The American people were tired and believed that it was time to focus our energy and resources on matters at home, but there was one issue that had not been resolved since the Civil War—race. The issue would shape American politics for the next 75 years.

When Dwight Eisenhower was elected president, *Plessy v. Ferguson* was the Supreme Court decision in force. The 1896 decision legalized state-mandated segregation. The segregation laws passed in the wake of this decision reflected the doctrine of "separate but equal." American citizens were separated by race in schools and public and private facilities, including government facilities, hotels, and restaurants. In several areas of the country, there were separate water fountains, bathrooms, and Black-only seating in the rear of the bus. Such laws, that started in the South after the Civil War and continued into the 1960s, were known as Jim Crow laws.

That was about to change. In Eisenhower's second year in office, *Brown v. Board of Education of Topeka, Kansas*, made its way to the Supreme Court. At issue, "Does the segregation of public education based solely on race violate the Equal Protection Clause of the Fourteenth Amendment?" The vote in the Supreme Court was 9—0, "The Court reasoned that the segregation of public education based on race instilled a sense of inferiority that had a hugely detrimental effect on the education and personal growth of African American children." The court ruled that there cannot be separate but equal schools in America. That meant desegregation of schools would be undertaken and a whole new set of issues to manage would be created going forward.

Desegregation sounds simple enough, but it required governments at the local and state levels to draft plans that showed how it would be accomplished. In several areas it represented dramatic social change being dictated from Washington. The court had decided based on the 14th amendment to our national constitution. The constitution also contains the 10th amendment that reserves powers for the states that are not enumerated as given to the federal government. States were about to test the limits of federal authority.

President Andrew Jackson purportedly said when the Supreme Court passed down a decision that was unfavorable to him in the case of *Worcester v. Georgia*: "John Marshall (who was the Chief Justice) has made his decision; now let him enforce it." The reality is that the Supreme Court does not have the power to enforce its decisions. That power resides with the executive who at this time was former five-star general Dwight David Eisenhower.

The reaction was swift and predictable to the *Brown v. Board of Education decision*. The Virginia Response stated: "If we can organize the Southern

States for massive resistance to this order, I think that in time the rest of the country will realize that racial integration is not going to be accepted in the South." As part of the resistance, Virginia Governor Thomas Bahnson Stanley appointed a commission in August 1954 to determine viable options for defying the *Brown decision*. The commission delivered three policy recommendations in November 1955:

- Laws concerning school attendance be amended so that no child would be required to attend an integrated school;
- Funds be allocated as tuition grants for parents who opposed schools comprised of white and Black students; and
- Local school boards be authorized to assign white and African American students to particular schools.

There was also a new doctrine developed to replace "separate by equal" that was called "interposition." The argument was the "state could interpose between an unconstitutional federal mandate and local authorities based on State Sovereignty." The battle lines were drawn for a showdown that pitted states' rights against federal authority.

In issues management context is always important because issues play out in the social and political environment in which they are managed. There are fact-based underpinnings to every opinion and position, so they should not be dismissed out of hand. Also, opinion is rarely changed by the use, or perceived use, of force. One of the great challenges of issues management is that at some point it becomes an art. President Eisenhower, whose leadership skills were homed in war, was well prepared to manage the complex issue he would soon face.

The civil rights movement focused on equality. When Rosa Parks refused to give up her seat on a bus to a white man in 1955 the movement found its voice. This would provide context for a boycott of the Montgomery, Alabama bus system led by Rev. Dr. Martin Luther King Jr. The boycott would help propel the case of *Browder v. Gayle* to be argued before the Supreme Court. The result was a striking down of discrimination laws on "city buses, trains and public waiting rooms." Gallup polling of this decision found that 70 percent of residents outside the South agreed with it while only 27 percent of those living in the South.

Politics of the issue was one side had the luxury of viewing the issue through the prism of right versus wrong while the other side saw it as imposing unwanted changes to their way of life.

According to the Miller Center at the University of Virginia:

> President Eisenhower did not fully support of the *Brown decision.* The president did not like dealing with racial issues and failed to speak out in favor of the court's ruling ... (but) Eisenhower did acknowledge his constitutional responsibility to uphold the Supreme Court's rulings.

The issue came to a head in 1957 at Central High School in Little Rock, Arkansas, when nine Black students were denied entry. Governor Orval Faubus had authorized the state's national guard to be used to deny Black students' entry into a public school. Eisenhower's instinct was to try to resolve the issue without much fanfare. The two met in Newport, Rhode Island, in early September, and the governor agreed to remove the national guard, but a violent mob soon replaced the national guard and tensions rose quickly. Eisenhower sent federal troops into the South for the first time since Reconstruction to enforce federal law.

Eisenhower would address the nation September 24, 1957, on his use of federal power, but not as a president who advocated for desegregation. Below are quotes from his speech:

1. **Tone:** "the sadness I feel in the action I was compelled today to make and the firmness with which I intend to pursue this course until the orders of the Federal Court at Little Rock can be executed without unlawful interference."
2. **Framing:** "under the leadership of demagogic extremists, disorderly mobs have deliberately prevented the carrying out of proper orders from a federal court."
3. **Problem:** "As you know, the Supreme Court of the United States has decided that separate public educational facilities for the races are inherently unequal; and therefore, compulsory school segregation laws are unconstitutional."

4. **Create Distance**: "Our personal opinions about the decision have no bearing on the matter of enforcement; the responsibility and authority of the Supreme Court to interpret the Constitution are very clear."

5. **Isolate Opposition**: "During the past several years, many communities in our Southern States have instituted public school plans for gradual progress in the enrollment and attendance of school children of all races in order to bring themselves into compliance with the law of the land."

6. **Federalism**: "The running of our school system and the maintenance of peace and order in each of our States are strictly local affairs and the Federal Government does not interfere except in very special cases."

7. **Reassurance**: "The proper use of the powers of the Executive Branch to enforce the orders of a Federal Court is limited to extraordinary and compelling circumstances."

8. **Forgiveness**: "I know that the overwhelming majority of the people in the South—including those of Arkansas and of Little Rock—are of good will, united in their efforts to preserve and respect the law even when they disagree with it."

9. **Offramp**: "If resistance to the Federal Court order ceases at once, the further presence of Federal troops will be unnecessary and the City of Little Rock will return to its normal habits of peace and order; and a blot upon the fair name and high honor of our nation in the world will be removed."

This is the finest example of threading the needle and framing the issue presented in this book. Eisenhower defined the narrative, positioned the issue, and provided the context in which the issue would be managed. He positioned himself not as a civil rights president who was on a crusade for equity and social justice, but as the rightful enforcer of federal law that included the decisions of the Supreme Court. He understood how this issue could spark tensions that could create much larger issues for the nation. Most importantly, he grasped that the issue was not "ripe" enough to be positioned as a national political issue because it was replete with "win-lose" options that the nation likely was not willing to face in 1957.

Eisenhower took a crisis that could have broken the nation and narrowed it down to a dispute instigated by hooligans in one city, which made it manageable. Additional significant civil rights legislation would have to wait another five years for Lyndon Johnson to address. What would change in just half a decade? Arguably, the mood of the country was shaped by events that followed including the assassination of John F. Kennedy.

Lessons

At Issue: The Supreme Court ruled that desegregation of schools was now the law of the land. This would not be accepted in states where racial segregation was woven into the fabric of their social order.

Lesson: President Eisenhower provides a master class in issues management by reframing a large and complicated issue as a small and manageable one.

1. **Read the Room**: Eisenhower accepted his responsibility as chief executive to enforce the decisions of the Supreme Court. He also recognized that it was time to send a message to those who opposed desegregation, but not to antagonize them to a point that could have torn apart our nation. In issues management, there is nothing wrong with half measures that accomplish the goal. Every battle does not have to be fought, and every skirmish does not need to end with the victor and the vanquished. The message from Eisenhower was clear: Block the doors of schools and federal troops will open them.

2. **Measure the Leash**: Eisenhower was a general and seen as a man of action, but as president, he realized that there are times when restraint is the better path. The public would have given Eisenhower the benefit of the doubt had he chosen to use force to accomplish boarder objectives, but Eisenhower knew that would not have ended the matter. Eisenhower used limited force that was enough to deescalate the crisis but not enough to cause another issue to grow in its place. In issues management, it is important to know how far to go and how far is too far. Remember that his initial goal was to lower the temperature and create a sense of calm. It was not to punish.

3. **Understand Context**: Fifty years after the *Brown decision*, in 2004, Americans were asked by Gallup whether educational opportunities for Black children were better or worse than they were 50 years earlier; 92 percent of whites answered better and 77 percent of Blacks agreed. It is difficult to impose social change from the top down. As a former general, Eisenhower understood strategy. He was trained to look at the entire field of play and assess how to best organize operationally to achieve objectives. Operationally, the government was not ready to go all in on civil rights in 1957 because the structure was not in place to manage the issue. When managing an issue, you need to assess how much stress your organization is able to accept and how many resources you are willing to expend to attain a goal. An organization that makes promises that it cannot keep and sets timelines it cannot abide by, is setting the table for failure.

4. **Frame the Action**: Eisenhower addressed the nation to make sure that there was clarity on the action he was going to take and a broad understanding of the goals he had set. He did it because he was about to take extraordinary action that could, were he to overplay his hand, have long-term devastating consequences on our nation. He did not want the American people to believe that he was sending an army to invade the South. In issues management, there are times when you will need to go to the microphone and explain the next steps and the reasoning behind them. This does not mean explaining every action in detail, just the consequential actions you are taking. This will help to short-circuit the spread of rumors, misinformation, and maintain organizational alignment.

5. **Correct Pace**: A lot of times, a leader's instinct is to act quickly and decisively in times of crisis. Sending federal troops immediately was not the best first move in this crisis. Eisenhower chose measured responses that were appropriate to the events on the ground. Avoid disturbing the hornets nest whenever possible. Instead, try to work around it. Eisenhower let state authorities play out their solution before he took any action to resolve the issue that required a show of federal power. When he did act, it was because he was left with no other choice. There are times when events call for

you to be proactive and other times when you need to be reactive. In both cases, events on the ground should dictate your response.

6. **Big Tent**: Bring as many people under your tent as possible early in the process of issues management. It would have been a huge mistake for Eisenhower to ignore Governor Orval Faubus of Arkansas in the early part of the crisis, because it would have created a conflict that was "lose-lose." Eisenhower knew that early in any conflict, there is an opportunity to move people onto his side by acknowledging the authority of the governor by inviting him to discuss the issue. It is rarely a best practice to make a list of enemies and friends at the start. How you manage the issue will shape opinion (support, opposition, neutral) throughout the process. It is good practice to keep your door open, at least a crack, at all times.

7. **Don't Escalate Without Cause**: Why fight a war when a battle will do? The decision to escalate, even when you have superior resources, should always be viewed as a major decision. Eisenhower could have nationalized this issue by going all in as a civil rights president. He also could have regionalized it by making it a state's rights issue. He could have personalized it by getting into a fight with the governor of Arkansas and forcing him to bend to his will. He followed none of those paths. Instead, he localized it, making it about a school and a small group of people within one city who were attempting to stop the enforcement of the federal laws, The key is to keep the issue in front of you and keep it as small and manageable as possible.

8. **Green Light—Red Light**: Eisenhower did not ignore the crisis in Little Rock because he knew that by allowing one state to use its national guard to deny access to Black children to enter a school, other states would read this as a green light to use similar force to resist desegregation. The use of force by states, as a viable option to achieve their goals, had to be taken off the table. When managing an issue, you are sending messages all the time and establishing new parameters by your actions. You need to be able to distinguish between "green light" and "red light" actions. The former gives permission and the latter creates restrictions.

9. **Someone Else's Shoes**: Any good issues manager will understand that there are genuine issues and concerns driving the actions of both

sides. A "win-win" resolution rarely ends successfully with the humiliation of either side. A corollary to this is to never assume that the other side is bluffing. Issues management is not a game of chicken. It is the serious work of bringing an issue to an acceptable resolution. The governor of Arkansas was presenting the real concerns of the people of his state. Eisenhower was smart not to minimize these concerns or embarrass the governor.

10. **How Change Works**: In Little Rock, Arkansas, Eisenhower not only calmed the waters of hate and division, but he also allowed the issue to continue playing out nationally. You manage the issue you have and try not to create new ones in the process. Eisenhower could only resolve the problem that had become a crisis in Little Rock. He managed the issue as well as possible in the times in which the issue presented itself. He did not use the issue as a springboard to solve other racial problems or to declare himself a civil right president. Americans were not ready to go that far, yet. Lasting change rarely happens in giant steps. Accept manageable change whenever possible. This is a good lesson to embrace.

11. **End Point**: Eisenhower spelled out under what conditions this crisis would end. He did not see his response as a mandate to institute dramatic change nationally. He did send a clear message that the federal government would enforce federal law when a state willfully disregards it. This opened the door for federal responses going forward in expanding civil rights in the United States. The crisis was over, and a clear message was sent. In issues management the results you get may seem underwhelming at times—more incremental than dramatic. What is important is that the right messages were sent to the right audiences; new boundaries were established to regulate future actions, and the process for achieving more broad-based change had begun. Effective issues management will include a clear definition of the terms under which you will declare the crisis is over. Eisenhower understood the amount of runway he was given and never ran out of it.

President Eisenhower would win a tactical victory in Little Rock using federal troops to help nine Black students enter what was formerly an all-white school. He also advanced strategy by sending a message to Black leaders, including Dr. King, that the federal government will have your back going forward. There would be a lot of violence and hardships that followed as the civil rights movement advanced in the United States. Eisenhower would not be listed as a champion of civil rights as a president, but the measured action he took set the stage for more dramatic action in the future.

Let us now explore how the first president born in the 20th century responded to a failed overthrown of the communist government of Cuba by examining John F. Kennedy's failure in the Bay of Pigs.

CHAPTER 5

Kennedy—Reframing the Issue

MSNBC host Joe Scarborough wrote:

> I see it all the time in politics. If a candidate gets caught in a lie, he quickly tries to change the subject by throwing more mud at his opponent. The mud keeps flying until some of the slanderous material sticks.

This is a tactic for some in issues management. A better approach is when something goes wrong, and it often will, then your best option is to recast it to reposition yourself to move forward. This is the lesson taught by John F. Kennedy after the failed Bay of Pigs invasion.

John Fitzgerald Kennedy's election in November 1960 would symbolize the first president born in the 20th century: Franklin Roosevelt was born in 1882; Harry Truman in 1884, and Dwight D. Eisenhower's birth year was 1890. Kennedy was born in 1917. He was a scion of a wealthy Boston family; Harvard educated, battle tested in World War II as the captain of a PT boat that was sunk by the Japanese, senator of the United States, and he was catholic. The first catholic ever elected president. He embodied a changing America that was far removed from the isolation of farm life and the oppression of early factory labor in cities.

The America of 1960 had a burgeoning middle class, and we were not at war. Kennedy embodied American optimism: young, handsome, urbane, well-educated, and witty with a beautiful wife and two young children. That was his brand and he used it to his advantage in politics.

Kennedy embraced the challenges of his generation. In his inaugural address, he proclaimed:

> Let the word go forth from this time and place, to friend and foe alike, that the torch has been passed to a new generation of Americans—born in this century, tempered by war, disciplined by a hard and bitter peace, proud of our ancient heritage, and unwilling to witness or permit the slow undoing of those human rights to which this nation has always been committed, and to which we are committed today at home and around the world.

He went on the frame his governing philosophy saying:

> And so, my fellow Americans, ask not what your country can do for you; ask what you can do for your country. My fellow citizens of the world, ask not what America will do for you, but what together we can do for the freedom of man.

This was the foundation of his government which at the time was called "Camelot"—the romanticized fictional kingdom ruled by King Arthur.

Kennedy faced two issues bubbling to the surface when he became president. The first was civil rights. The movement had started in the South in the late 1950s. The voice and face of civil rights in America was Rev. Dr. Martin Luther King Jr. King, a Baptist minister who believed that nonviolence was the true path to social justice. He led marches throughout the South and had been arrested over 30 times. With each arrest, he raised public consciousness of the plight of civil rights in America. During Kennedy's 1,000 days in office, King would rise to national prominence culminating with his "I Have a Dream" speech in Washington DC in 1963 where he expressed his desire that his children be judged by the "content of their character not by the color of their skin."

The other issue was the spread of communism. The Truman Doctrine focused on stopping the advance of communism into Greece and Turkey. He would go to war to stop it from dominating the Korean Peninsula in 1950. The Eisenhower Doctrine stated that the United States would "secure and protect the territorial integrity and political independence of such nations, requesting such aid against overt armed aggression from any nation controlled by international communism." Under Eisenhower, communism was branded as the "Red Menace," and communist sympathizers were rooted out of society. Several artists and movie stars were "blacklisted" after they were brought before the House Un-American Activities Committee to testify. Concerns about communism were not lost on Kennedy who had served in the Senate with Sen. Joe McCarthy, who as a senator lead a purge of communism in the United States.

When World War II ended, a new enemy of freedom began to take form, flex its muscle, and spread throughout the world—communism. Most of the economies in the world were destroyed by the war. As they rebuilt, several began to consider alternatives to the economic systems they had before the war began.

On March 5, 1946, then former British prime minister Winston Churchill gave his "Sinews of Peace" speech at Westminster College in Fulton, Missouri. He attended at the invitation of President Harry S. Truman, whose home state was Missouri. He started by defining the new world order: "The United States stands at this time at the pinnacle of world power. It is a solemn moment for the American Democracy. For with primacy in power is also joined an awe-inspiring accountability to the future." Throughout our history, the United States had, in the main, kept to itself and let other nations lead the world. This would change after World War II, and Churchill was here to pass the baton.

Churchill then warned:

Nobody knows what Soviet Russia and its Communist international organization intends to do in the immediate future ... From Stettin in the Baltic to Trieste in the Adriatic, an iron curtain has descended across the Continent. Behind that line lie all the capitals of the ancient states of Central and Eastern Europe. Warsaw, Berlin, Prague, Vienna, Budapest, Belgrade, Bucharest and Sofia, all these famous cities and the populations around them lie in what I must call the Soviet sphere, and all are subject in one form or another, not only to Soviet influence but to a very high and, in many cases, increasing measure of control from Moscow.

Churchill would coin the term "Cold War" that would frame the geo-political landscape for the next 50 years.

As the curtain went down on World War II, it rose on the spread of communism. The Eastern Bloc in Europe was under Soviet control. In 1949, a revolution in China established communism under Mao Zedong. Our policy was containment, supported by the "domino theory" that was playing out before our eyes on the global stage. In 1950, we entered a shooting war in Korea to stop the spread of communism. It ended in a stalemate. Containment strategy could require us to fight a series of proxy wars because both superpowers had nuclear weapons, and the death and destruction of a hot war with the USSR were unthinkable.

In issues management, the torch is often passed from leader to leader before the problem is solved. There was no "solution" to communism in the post-World War II world. Policies were put in place only to contain it. At some point, a leader would face "problem creep" where containment fails, and the issue has arrived at the doorstep, and more aggressive action needs to be put on the table.

Cuba was the vacation spot on the Caribbean for the wealthy in the early 20th century. *Smithsonian Magazine* put it this way:

> Cuba's reputation as an exotic and permissive playground came to light in the 1920s, when the country became a favorite destination for robber barons and bohemians. Scions like the Whitneys and the Biltmores, along with luminaries such as New York City Mayor Jimmy "Beau James" Walker, flocked to Cuba for winter bouts of gambling, horse racing, golfing and country-clubbing.

By the 1950s it was a tourist destination. "Havana was then what Las Vegas has become," says Louis Perez, a Cuba historian at the University of North Carolina at Chapel Hill, as cited in *Smithsonian*. It attracted mafia kingpins such as Meyer Lansky and Santo Trafficante, who were evading a national investigation into organized crime. In Cuba, "they could continue their stock trade of gambling, drugs and prostitution, as long as they paid off government officials."

The *Smithsonian* article goes on the point out:

> By the late '50s, U.S. commercial interests included 90 percent of Cuban mines, 80 percent of its public utilities, 50 percent of its railways, 40 percent of its sugar production and 25 percent of its bank deposits—some $1 billion in total. American influence extended into the cultural realm, as well. Cubans grew accustomed to the luxuries of American life. They drove American cars, owned TVs, watched Hollywood movies and shopped at Woolworth's department store. The youth listened to rock and roll, learned English in school, adopted American baseball and sported American fashions.

The Cuban government was corrupt and its society increasingly decadent. When sugar prices fell in the late 1950s, Cuba's substantial middle class felt the pain. Change was in the air. Those who felt that Cuba had lost its national identity and those who felt the government was irreparably corrupt framed the issue for the Cuban people. In 1957, the first shots of revolution were fired. The Cuban people turned to a wealthy scion of the landowning class—Fidel Castro—who was both a nationalist and corruption fighter to bring the changes needed to restore Cuban identity. In January 1959, Castro took power in Cuba and set it on a course to become the first communist nation in the western hemisphere.

Cubans who saw the trajectory of Castro's "reforms" fled the island nation. Many came to the United States and settled in Florida. It is estimated that about 500,000 people, many of whom were professionals and business owners, fled Cuba and settled in Miami during the early years of Castro's rule.

The revolution that precipitated Castro's rise to power destroyed Cuba's western business model. What was left was a Las Vegas without resorts, gambling, and entertainment. The tourism industry quickly dried up. The country was left with a "sugar crop" based economy. Needing friends and economic support, Castro turned to Nikita Khrushchev and the Soviet Union.

Kennedy had been briefed early in his administration by the Central Intelligence Agency that Cuba was fast becoming a communist client state. The agency had prepared plans to train Cuban refugees into an army that would invade Cuba and overthrow Castro.

In April of 1961, President Kennedy enjoyed an 83 percent approval rating. He certainly had political capital to expend, and the rewards for overthrowing the first communist satellite state in the Western Hemisphere would be enormous and mark a clear victory for democracy and freedom in the ongoing Cold War.

There are similarities to Truman making his decision to drop the bomb on Japanese civilians. Truman assumed it would end the war quickly. He was correct. Kennedy assumed the successful invasion would strike a blow to the expansion of communism internationally. He was wrong. The difference in the two decisions was Truman knew for certain that he could drop the bomb, but Kennedy has no assurances that the invasion would be successful.

The Kennedy Library archives the Bay of Pigs this way:

> The original invasion plan called for two air strikes against Cuban air bases. A 1,400-man invasion force would disembark under cover of darkness and launch a surprise attack. Paratroopers dropped in advance of the invasion would disrupt transportation and repel Cuban forces. Simultaneously, a smaller force would land on the east coast of Cuba to create confusion.

The invasion was a disaster. The Central Intelligence Agency backed force was routed on the beach. Kennedy was embarrassed knowing the political fallout could be substantial. Kennedy would reframe the failure this way:

1. **Define the Enemy**: It is clear that the forces of communism are not to be underestimated, in Cuba or anywhere else in the world. The advantages of a police state—its use of mass terror and arrests to prevent the spread of free dissent—cannot be overlooked by those who expect the fall of every fanatic tyrant.
2. **Provide a Rationale for Action**: Is clear that this Nation, in concert with all the free nations of this hemisphere, must take an ever closer and more realistic look at the menace of external Communist intervention and domination in Cuba. The American people are not

complacent about Iron Curtain tanks and planes less than 90 miles from their shore.

3. **Recast the Nature of Warfare**: It is clearer than ever that we face a relentless struggle in every corner of the globe that goes far beyond the clash of armies or even nuclear armaments.... The nuclear armaments are there. But they serve primarily as the shield behind which subversion, infiltration, and a host of other tactics steadily advance, picking off vulnerable areas one by one in situations which do not permit our own armed intervention.

The nature of war had changed in the age of nuclear weapons, and Kennedy would double down on his failure at Bay of Pigs by authorizing, a covert "coordinated program of political, psychological, military, sabotage, and intelligence operations, as well as proposed assassination attempts on key political leaders, including Castro." This ongoing hostility toward Cuba would set the stage for the Cuban Missile Crisis in October 1962.

Lessons

At Issue: Cuba, an island nation 90 miles off the coast of Key West, Florida, was moving into the communist orbit. This would provide the USSR with a base from which communism could be spread into central and South America and target U.S. cities with nuclear-tipped missiles. Kennedy authorized an invasion that failed.

Lesson: President Kennedy shows us the value of reframing failure and owning missteps to maintain credibility to help regain control of the narrative.

1. **Strategy Outpacing Operations**: Liberating Cuba was a sound strategic goal for an American president in 1961. The regime was not yet fully established but the threat was clear. The problem was that goals must be matched to operational capabilities in order to be achieved. The Bay of Pigs invasion had too many loose ends and unfounded assumptions from the start. In managing an issue, you need to make sure that you have the capability to do what you claim must be done.

If not, then you need to restate your goals and redefine your strategy to align with your capabilities.

2. **Failure Starts at the Beginning**: The CIA plan contained a lot of assumptions that needed to work perfectly for the mission to succeed. When the first piece, the air strike, failed, the entire mission was doomed. Most well-crafted issues management plans depend on having a successful first step. Your time, effort, and focus should be on doing whatever is needed to make your first move the right move. There is one starting line in issues management, and there are few good opportunities for restarts. Once out of the gate, you are in a dynamic environment where other factors come into play that can quickly determine the success or failure of your plan.

3. **Question Advice**: When you visit a surgeon to discuss a problem, do not be surprised if her solution includes surgery. The CIA is in the business of covert operations and often uses surrogates to carry out its missions. The agency was only in existence since 1947 when it was advising Kennedy to invade Cuba using Cuban refugees. It was looking to make a name for itself after its initial success in Guatemala in the early 1950s. Understanding power relationships when managing an issue is especially important. Sometimes a senior person will be deferred to based solely on the position held. Other times, the people who drive issues management assume powers they do not have in normal business operations. Having a strategy that is bought into at every level should control the management of any issue—period. It should include a well-defined chain of command and decision-making structure.

4. **Pulling Rank**: Allen Dulles was head of the CIA and was instrumental in advising Kennedy to move forward with the invasion. Dulles was a legendary figure in Washington. Kennedy would later say, "I probably made a mistake in keeping Allen Dulles on. It is not that Dulles is not a man of great ability. He is. But I have never worked with him and therefore I can't estimate his meaning when he tells me things." When you have consultants hired to help with issues management, always keep in mind that you are the most knowledgeable person in the room most of the time. The consultant's job is to make sure you have a workable strategy and have not missed any steps in

sequencing activities and are doing a correct assessment of what is happening in the field.

5. **Avoid "Lose-Lose" Outcomes**: Things will go wrong, and mistakes will happen, but disasters trump all of that in the minds of the public. Signing on to the "half-baked" CIA plan to invade Cuba showed questionable judgment on the part of Kennedy. The plan's spectacular failure called into question his competence. Kennedy was skillful in managing the fallout in the wake of the disaster, but he still put his reputation at risk. In issues management, you never want to roll the dice on the future of your organization when implementing a plan. Any plan can fail. If your plan fails, then your job is to make sure that the damage to the organization is not fatal.

6. **Play the Odds**: In the movie "Dumb and Dumber," Jim Carey's character asks if he has a chance with the woman of his dreams. The answer is "one in a million." He responds, "So you're telling me there's a chance?" Failure is always an option; therefore, any response to an issue must include what you do if things do not work out as planned. Kennedy was quick to respond, and his response was on-point and excellent at reading the room. He did not run away from failure expecting it to be forgotten. He hit it head on. When things do not go right, that is the time honesty and candor are most needed.

7. **Own Failure**: Kennedy skillfully won the initial public relations skirmish by not asking for forgiveness in his press conference after the failure at the Bay of Pigs. Instead, he used it as a teaching moment to stress that the threat of communism is real and pervasive, and that the nature of conflict had changed in the nuclear age. Actions do not have to be successful to be accepted by the public. Aiming high and coming up a little short is often an acceptable outcome. Handled properly, you won't get blamed for trying and failing if you frame it in a larger context to point out that the objective was not reached, but good things happened along the way.

8. **Unexpected Consequences**: Cuba won the Bay of Pigs invasion in more ways than just on the battlefield. Cuba was now a victim of U.S. hostile aggression and intervention in its national affairs. By invading Cuba, Kennedy made the case to the USSR that we were

hostile neighbors hell-bent on Cuba's destruction. This opened the door for the USSR to send more arms and aid to Cuba. It also left the United States, at least initially, having no public case to make to stop USSR from arming Cuba. Creating a victim within the context of managing an issue is rarely a good idea.

9. **Doubling Down**: The failure at the Bay of Pigs gave rise to "Operation Mongoose" as a failed invasion now shifted focus to covert operations. Kennedy seemed committed to ridding the Western Hemisphere of communism. Moving to covert actions not only kept the conflict going but opened a new front. It also provided our enemies with a public relations coup: The world's leading democracy cannot be fully trusted or believed. Retreat from transparency is usually not a good move in issues management because it can create problems in other areas that can tarnish reputation.

10. **Checkmate**: One outcome of the Bay of Pigs was that it tied Kennedy's hands from undertaking military action against Cuba in its aftermath. The invasion failed to achieve its objective, and it also took a lot of other options off the table when it failed. There are moves in checkers and chess that offer short-term success while at the same time setting the stage for your ultimate defeat. Our failures in the early 1960s set the table for more than 60 years of hostility toward Cuba. In issues management, try to understand what other pieces are in play and may fall as a result of every move you make before you make it.

11. **Morphing**: On the heels of the botched Bay of Pigs invasion was the Cuban Missile Crisis. Here Kennedy would face down the very real possibility of nuclear war with the USSR. The communists were building nuclear missile silos in Cuba and preparing to load weapons. This 13-day standoff shook the world. It was resolved in the favor of the United States in the near term, but not until several strategic concessions were made to the USSR by the United States regarding our defense posture in Europe. Once the first domino falls, it takes others with it. The fallout of failure can happen down the road when it can come back as a much bigger and more dangerous issue.

There were several other outcomes that could be traced to what happened at the Bay of Pigs and the Cuban Missile Crisis that followed. After coming so close to a nuclear war, a partial nuclear test ban treaty was signed. Also, with a better understanding of communism's ability to metastasize, the United States would send billions of dollars in foreign aid to Latin America. This would become the new normal of the Cold War, where guns were replaced with dollars to achieve national security goals.

Next, we will turn to the presidency of Lydon Baines Johnson and look at what happens when a belief is so steadfastly adhered to that it sinks a presidency.

CHAPTER 6

Johnson—Abandoning Your Strengths

Former UCLA basketball coaching legend John Wooden said this about change: "Failure isn't fatal, but failure to change might be." The ability to adjust and adapt as situations change is imperative to successful issues management. Lyndon B. Johnson, one the most effective presidents in passing legislation, clung to his position in Vietnam for too long, and it would cost him his presidency in the end.

The presidency of Lyndon Baines Johnson of Texas began following the tragic assassination of John F. Kennedy in Dallas, Texas, on November 22, 1963. The contrast between the two men could not have been greater. Kennedy was young and handsome; Johnson was 55 years old when he assumed office but appeared to be much older than Kennedy, who was 46 years old when he died. Kennedy had a patrician accent and was Harvard educated. Johnson had a West Texas drawl and was a graduate of Texas State University, although he did have a law degree from Georgetown University.

Kennedy was a man of great wealth and privilege who provided America with glimpses into the world of the rich and famous. He vacationed at his family's compound in Hyannisport, Massachusetts, where he sailed a yacht and played touch football on the compound's extensive lawn. Kennedy was married to Jacqueline Lee Bouvier, who was the daughter of a wealthy stockbroker. Jackie graduated from Miss Porter's boarding school and Vassar College and took a year to study in Paris. She studied ballet, spoke fluent French, and was an accomplished equestrian rider. They were an elegant couple. Their circle of friends was vast and included movie stars as well as the "who's who" of the uber-wealthy in society. Their two children, Caroline and John (John John), were right out of central casting and projected the image of the joy and chaos that comes with raising young children in the White House.

The Miller Center at the University of Virginia highlights Johnson's impoverished background and rise to power. Johnson was born on a farm and raised in Johnson City, Texas, which is west of Austin and even today boasts of a population of under 2,000. The first office he held was president of his six-person high school graduating class. Johnson had a brief teaching career where he earned $1,530 a year. His first political job was as an aide to Congressman Richard Kleberg, where, "His drive, ambition, and competence made him stand out among the young people in Washington at that time." His wife was Claudia "Lady Bird" Johnson (nee Taylor), whom he married in 1934. She came from a modestly successful family, who had enough money for her to be considered a socialite, and she was well-educated for women of her time as a graduate of the University of Texas. She planned to use her degree to pursue a career in journalism. The Johnsons had two children, Linda Bird and Lucy Baines, who were 19 and 16 years old, respectively, when Johnson became president.

Johnson was a skilled politician, hard worker, policy wonk, and driven to succeed. He understood how to work the levers of power in Washington to get things done. He was hell-bent on being a very consequential president, which was his dream since high school. According to Miller Center:

> Johnson's ascent to power (in the Senate) was startling; by the end of his first term, he was one of the most powerful senators in America. He used strategies that had enabled his fast climb in the House: wooing powerful members, angling for spots on important committees, and outworking everyone.

In his address to Congress on November 27, 1963, Johnson's issues management skills were on full display as he showed a complete understanding of the challenges he faced:

1. **Captured the Moment**: "All I have I would have given gladly not to be standing here today," going on the say, "He (Kennedy) lives on

in the mind and memories of mankind. He lives on in the hearts of his countrymen."

2. **Defined the Mission**: "No words are strong enough to express our determination to continue the forward thrust of America that he began."

3. **Affirmed his Mandate**: "[T]his is no time for delay. It is a time for action—strong, forward-looking action ..." adding "The need is here. The need is now."

Lyndon Johnson would enjoy the highest approval rating overall (74.2 percent) of any president, from Harris S. Truman through Joe Biden, when serving out the last 14 months of Kennedy's term according to Gallup. Johnson had skillfully promised to fulfill Kennedy's agenda. As a symbol of this pledge, he retained Kennedy's entire cabinet which included Robert F. (Bobby) Kennedy, the brother of the late president.

Bobby Kennedy was neither a close confidant nor a trusted adviser to Johnson, but Johnson understood politics enough to know that the American people were not ready for sunset on Kennedy's "Camelot" administration. He also did not want to create a "Kennedy Faction" within the Democratic Party that could interfere with the passage of his ambitious agenda.

There are three important lessons here in issues management: First lesson is if you inherit goodwill then use it to your advantage. The second lesson is a new leader does not necessitate a new team. Third lesson is don't go out of your way to create enemies when there is little upside and a lot of potential downside.

Johnson was a master of the legislative process and started using his political goodwill and spending his political capital to tackle big issues. He told Congress: "We have talked long enough in this country about equal rights. We have talked for one hundred years or more. It is time now to write the next chapter, and to write it in the books of law." In 1957, Johnson, as majority leader, passed the Civil Rights Act through the Senate. "To see Lyndon Johnson, get that bill through, almost vote by vote," said Pulitzer Prize-winning LBJ biographer Robert Caro, "is to see not only legislative power but legislative genius."

On May 3, 1963, the headline in *The New York Times* read: "DOGS AND HOSES REPULSE NEGROES AT BIRMINGHAM; 3 Students Bitten in Second Day of Demonstrations Against Segregation; 250 MARCHERS SEIZED." President Kennedy announced in a televised news conference that he was sending civil rights legislation to Congress. That night Medgar Evers, head of the Mississippi chapter of the National Association for the Advancement of Colored People (NAACP) was murdered in his driveway. In August, Rev. King delivered his powerful "I have a Dream" speech in Washington. It drew a quarter million people. In Birmingham, Alabama, in September, there was more violence when four young Black girls were killed in the bombing of their church. Politically, these events did not move the needle in Congress to pass Kennedy's legislation.

Johnson seized the initiative once he became president, positioning the passage of civil rights legislation as a homage to the late president. He would leverage his high approval ratings and his knowledge of the legislative process to get the job done. Johnson would undertake a transformation of America that would rival FDR's "New Deal" 30 years earlier as he nationalized the civil rights issue into a political crusade.

In a commencement speech at the University of Michigan, on May 22, 1964, Johnson framed his domestic legislative agenda to create the "Great Society." The goal he set was to "end poverty and racial injustice." His primary tool would be the federal government providing money and setting national standards and the states implementing the plan. Johnson signed into law the Civil Rights Act of 1964 on July 2.

Later that year, Johnson asked Congress to declare a "War on Poverty." It did, and new federal programs and federal dollars started to flow out of Washington into cities, schools, jobs programs, anti-poverty programs, housing programs, public assistance, and many other initiatives focused on helping the poor. Government would, over the decades that followed, spend trillions of dollars to eliminate poverty.

The issues management lesson here is about timing the issue. Johnson had a mandate to act, and he used it to focus on civil rights. He had goodwill. External events created a solid foundation on which to act, and he was a master of the legislative process. Knowing when to act is as important as what you want to do or the goals you set.

Johnson was about to make a critical mistake by believing that he could pursue parallel goals simultaneously without exhausting his resources and diminishing his goodwill. In issues management, priorities are always changing, and by setting two long-term goals, you always run the risk of not being able to adequately address brushfires or other challenges when they arise. Johnson was about to learn this lesson.

In his address to a Joint Session of Congress on November 27, 1963, Johnson almost prophetically stated:

> In this age when there can be no losers in peace and no victors in war, we must recognize the obligation to match national strength with national restraint. We must be prepared at the same time for both the confrontation of power and the limitation of power.

Had he lived by these words, he likely would have been reelected in 1968 instead of being forced not to seek another term as Vietnam began to manage him.

Vietnam was a small country in Southeast Asia that would be an issue for four American presidents starting with Eisenhower and ending with Nixon. Strategy was based on the belief that communism would spread based on the "domino theory." The Geneva Accords in 1954 crafted a solution for Vietnam, after France withdrew from the country following military defeat, that closely followed what had happened in Korea. Vietnam would be divided at the 17th parallel creating North Vietnam and South Vietnam. In the north nationalism was strong and was embodied in Ho Chi Minh who was a "communist" leading a peasant people with the support of the USSR and China. The South would become a proxy nation where an effort was made by Western powers to build a Western-like government and economy, using the examples of West Berlin and Japan after World War II. The goal of the Geneva Plan was to have a vote on uniting the two parts of the country into one nation. The vote never happened. Instead, western nations invested heavily in Vietnam leading to corruption. Like with Cuba, guerilla insurgencies would rise to undo corruption and restore nationalism. This insurgency in South Vietnam became known as the Viet Cong. The United States would find itself right in the middle of what could be described as a civil war for two decades.

U.S. involvement began under Eisenhower, expanded under Kennedy, and now the ball was in Johnson's court. It is common in issues management to inherit issues that your predecessors have not resolved. The problem leaders face in this situation is they usually do not accept the status quo and instead choose to add to the strategy. Strategy reassessment with a change in leadership is a good idea, but it should be undertaken with an operational and tactical capabilities reassessment. In Vietnam, it was always assumed that it was a military problem. A sober analysis of the issue would have found that the bigger problem was a corrupt government that lacked popular support and the limitations of force to alter national fervor. In 1965, fresh off of his landslide election, President Johnson said: "I am not going to lose Vietnam." This was a big leap from Kennedy's policy. Johnson's strategy was initially "containment," which meant that communism would be stopped in Vietnam by whatever means and at whatever cost were necessary. Every president since Franklin Roosevelt had their war to fight or end. Vietnam would be Johnson's to fight. He would stop the spread of communism, unlike those who came before him, and create a functioning democracy.

A common mistake made by leaders is "me-too." They don't want to be the one to stop "progress" on an issue. In the process, they often misread the issue, fail to assess progress made to date, and do not consider how the issue has changed over time. Johnson would operate from a false assumption that Vietnam was a problem that could be fixed by introducing overwhelming military force.

In 1959, the United States had 760 troops in Vietnam; in 1963, the number grew to 16,300; in 1965, it stood at 183,300; and it topped out in 1968 at 536,100. This upward trajectory spanned three presidencies. The issues management assessment should have been to answer whether things were improving, staying the same or getting worse as more resources were committed.

The issue began to change as the public perceived a lack of clear goals and measurable progress. It started on campuses in 1964 with protests at Columbia, Berkeley, California, and Yale University. In May 1966, there was a march in Washington DC that would draw nearly 10,000 protesters. Singer/songwriter Tom Paxton would mock Johnson with these lyrics: "And Lyndon Johnson told the nation, have no fear of escalation,

I am trying everyone to please. Though it isn't really war, we're sending fifty thousand more, to help save Vietnam from the Vietnamese." The song was asking questions that Johnson had ignored.

In the Phil Ochs song "Draft Dodgers Rag," he captured the sentiments of the Vietnam generation who were being called to fight the war: "Ooh, I hate Chou En Lai and I hope he dies, But one thing you gotta see, That someone's gotta go over there, And that someone isn't me." There was a growing political movement in the United States against the war in Vietnam. Candidates for office were beginning to run on antiwar platforms. Johnson responded slowly. Americans were moving away from the long-held belief that we are always the good guys riding to the rescue. They could not figure out who was being rescued in Vietnam and questioned whether it was worth the price we were paying in blood and treasure.

The ground was shifting under Johnson's feet. Vietnam was the first televised war. Every night the major television networks, cable news did not exist at that time, showed the horrible realities of Vietnam. This made it difficult for Johnson to control the narrative.

As a result between July and October 1967, according to Roper, the number of Americans who thought we should just get out of Vietnam grew to 44 percent from 24 percent. The poll also reported that disapproval of Johnson's handling of the war stood at 60 percent on September 7, 1967. Interestingly, the loss of support was not among the young who were protesting the war but rather among older Americans, many of whom were veterans of World War II and Korea.

As an issues manager, Johnson focused only on the outcome and ignored reassessing and rethinking the issue. He tried everything tactically, changing generals, adding troops, sending more lethal arms, but tactics cannot cover up flawed strategic assumptions. He was fighting a peasant insurgency using the most lethal army ever fielded, and he could never seem to achieve a clear advantage.

In January 1968, the Tet Offensive shocked the American people. The insurgency was able to wage war in Saigon—the capitol of South Vietnam. On February 27, 1968, after his visit to Vietnam, CBS News anchorman Walter Cronkite, the most trusted name in news declared, that the "conflict would not end in victory but rather in stalemate." Johnson had lost control of the narrative.

A president who vowed he would not lose Vietnam had lost the hearts and minds of many of the American people. In the New Hampshire primary in 1968, Johnson faced an antiwar Democrat. As reported in *Politico*: "Sen. Eugene McCarthy (D-Minn.), a critic of President Lyndon B. Johnson's Vietnam policies, captured 42 percent of the vote in New Hampshire's first-in-the-nation Democratic presidential primary." Johnson was a savvy enough politician to know that no matter how hard he worked or how much money he spent, the 1968 campaign would be about the Vietnam War.

On March 31, 1968, in an address to the American people, Johnson said:

> With America's sons in the fields far away, with America's future under challenge right here at home, with our hopes and the world's hopes for peace in the balance every day, I do not believe that I should devote an hour or a day of my time to any personal partisan causes or to any duties other than the awesome duties of this office—the presidency of this country, Accordingly, I shall not seek, and I will not accept, the nomination of my party for another term as your president.

It was over for the most skilled legislator in our history to become president.

Lessons

At Issue: President Johnson was all-in on Vietnam with flawed strategy to achieve unrealistic goals.

Lesson: Going all-in with a strategy can provide the richest rewards, but also can position you for the greatest failure.

1. **Unrealistic Outcome**: Issues managers, and the strategy they create, set the terms by which their plans will be judged. Johnson set the bar high, leaving ultimate victory the only measurement of his success. Be careful not to oversell what you can achieve by understanding your operational capabilities.

2. **Limitations**: Power has limits. Having superior resources does not guarantee success. The United States had the greatest and best equipped armed forces in the world, but that did not ensure victory against a peasant army fighting for a cause. Johnson's belief in force as his primary tool took other options off the table. A one-dimensional strategy usually requires constant scrutiny because it is built on a set of assumptions that do not respond well to change.

3. **Flawed Strategy**: There are points in issues management where you need to be open to the idea that what you are doing is not working, and doing more of it is not likely to alter that result. Failed strategy is like dominoes falling. First, you don't get results. Next, key people begin to question what you are doing. Then, support begins to erode. Lastly, you lose control of the narrative.

4. **Reading the Room**: Having a good inner circle of advisers you trust to speak truth to power is a best practice in issues management. Opposition starts with a whisper. Best practice is having key people assessing these whispers. In Johnson's case, every failure or atrocity committed in Vietnam served to nourish the opposition that grew into a more widely accepted point of view.

5. **Expending Political Capital**: Every leader has limited political capital to expend. Johnson was a master legislator, but in the process of passing legislation, there are always a few eggs broken. This creates enemies who sought an opportunity for payback. As Johnson expended his political capital on Vietnam, he became weaker. When goodwill runs low, those who believe they can gain by taking a different course are emboldened to do so. An old friend once shared this lesson about politics: "Your friends don't elect you; your enemies defeat you." Sound advice.

6. **Never Make it Personal**: Vietnam to Johnson was a personal challenge. Issues management is about the execution of a viable strategy. We all have blind spots, and leaders need to endeavor to recognize areas in which they are not fully objective. Best practice is having members of your team who will point them out to you. Another flaw in making an issue personal is seeing the issue through an "us versus them" lens. It is NEVER a good practice to cross-over into

emotional and visceral responses when managing issues. Follow your plan. Stay objective.

7. **Time**: People want the results they have been promised. Each time Johnson increased troop levels, expanded strategy, or introduced more lethal tactics into Vietnam, he was making a promise to the American people—we now have in place the "secret sauce" and are ready to win. In issues management, we have stressed the importance of the first move being the right move. There is a corollary, which is making sure that your first small victory is not delayed. The lesson is that when you are managing an issue you are always on the clock to produce concrete results. Time is not your friend.

8. **The Externals**: At each level of media coverage, your strategy needs to be assessed. What works in your community, where they know you, may not play out the same way with a national audience. Vietnam was the first war reported nightly on television. The challenge was for Johnson's team to stay ahead of the story to make sure they were controlling the narrative. They became overwhelmed as events outflanked messaging which opened two fronts: fighting in Vietnam and managing public opinion.

9. **Avoid Exaggeration**: As early as 1965, as reported in *The New York Times*, Secretary of Defense Robert McNamara said at a press conference: "In the past four and one-half years, the Vietcong, the Communist insurgency in the South, have lost 89,000 men." Exaggeration was commonplace in government reports of progress in Vietnam. At some point, when you are trying to force a narrative that can't be sustained, you lose credibility. The narrative needs to comport with reality. Always assume the truth will come out and assess the damage it will do when it does.

10. **Enough Rope**: The American people gave Johnson what he said he needed with the promise of success. He got more troops, and he got more money. In issues management, there always comes a point where you are expected to deliver the results you promised. In every step of this process, balancing expectations becomes more difficult without real progress to report. There will always be enough rope in which to become entangled, so never confuse the amount of rope

you are given with the level of support you assume you have for what you are doing. Focus on results.

11. **Clarity Always**: The rationale for Vietnam changed over time, and with it support ebbed and flowed. Stating objectives and achieving them is critical to success. Goals should be as clearly stated as possible. Murkiness is the enemy of effective communication. In Johnson's case, the deeper he went into Vietnam, the less clear and more confusing the rationale became for being there. Events on the ground began to create their own truth. This is why every issue has a finite lifespan in which to be managed.

12. **Context**: In an earlier speech, Johnson admitted that the nature of war had changed. He did not follow his own advice. Vietnam was not World War II or Korea, where huge armies met on the field of battle. Vietnam was skirmishes, and we did not build our army to fight that kind of war. The American people figured this out over time. This is why a tactical assessment is important before you implement strategy.

13. **Perception Is Reality**. The perception of an issue often defines it. You can win every engagement but still be perceived as losing because people don't believe you are winning. Most of the major battles in Vietnam were won by the Americans, but reporting often focuses on failures and setbacks Explaining failure is a much more daunting task than selling success. In issues management, it is important to project purpose and commitment and, more importantly, faith and confidence that the strategy is working. The minute you act like you are losing, then you are in fact losing.

14. **Winners and Losers**: Assessing the interests of stakeholders is an especially important aspect of issues management. Vietnam was a poor man's war. Those fighting it, in the main, were from the groups with the least power in our society. On the other side were college kids, who were the first to protest the war, who had, at least in their minds, the most to lose by going to Vietnam. The Vietnam protests began with anger and concern but spread because of frustration and disillusionment.

15. **Words End**: There comes a time in managing an issue when you end up where you began. There are no credible arguments left for

you to use. This happened to Johnson when he realized the 1968 election would be a referendum on his handling of the Vietnam War and he was powerless to change that reality. At some point in issues management, you run out of words to say, and there are no more constituencies to win over. At this point, you have lost.

Lyndon Johnson was a consequential president who had a blind spot on one large issue. In the end, money and programs alone could not solve poverty, and weapons and troops could not change the hearts and minds of the people of Vietnam. The main lessons to be learned from Johnson and Vietnam are the dangers of losing control of the narrative. When managing an issue, you must tack when the wind shifts. Johnson had gotten himself in so deep that he had no room to tack to ride out the shift in public opinion. He wanted something too much that he could never really control, and he doubled down on a flawed strategy. In the end, he had expended all his political capital, and he knew he could no longer manage the issue to his advantage. He would return to his Texas ranch to live out his life.

Let's now turn to Richard M. Nixon to learn how the most powerful man in the world can lose the loyalty of his team and ability to govern.

CHAPTER 7

Nixon—Losing Credibility

French poet Joseph Roux wrote: "Solitude vivifies; isolation kills." In issues management, adequate time should be devoted to reflection but none to self-pity. Do not lament why something is going wrong. Fix it. Issues management demands sustained engagement, and success is never guaranteed. Richard M. Nixon would choose denial, avoidance, and self-isolation during the Watergate crisis, and he paid the highest price.

In 1964, "LBJ won 44 states and 61.1 percent of the popular vote, the highest percentage since the election of 1820." His popularity was high. He had successfully cultivated his appeal by promising to implement the agenda that John F. Kennedy had left incomplete, and he leveraged this positioning to move a dramatic domestic agenda through Congress. His skill in controlling the legislative process was unmatched, and he promised even bigger things in his second term.

America between 1965 and 1968 became an angrier and more impatient nation. In civil rights, the nonviolent movement of Dr. King was being challenged by new Black leaders who demanded the pace of change quicken and that violence should be considered as an appropriate tool. On February 21, 1965, former Nation of Islam leader Malcolm X was assassinated in New York. On March 7, 1965, on the Edmund Pettis Bridge in Selma, Alabama, about 600 Black protesters were violently attacked by police using dogs, clubs, and water cannon. In 1966, Stokely Carmichael assumed leadership of the Southern Christian Leadership Conference and the Black Panther Party was founded in Oakland, California. Many in the militant arm of the civil rights movement, who embraced Black Power, also adopted a form of Marxism. Cities across America burned as race riots erupted in Watts, Harlem, Atlanta, and Detroit to name a few. Although Johnson continued to pass legislation to aid Black America, the change was not coming fast enough for some.

The war in Vietnam gave rise to the antiwar movement on campuses across America. This movement initially followed King's lead and focused on marches and sit-ins, but like the civil rights movement, it too began to devolve into violence. The military draft was calling up 40,000 young men per month, and the demand for troops by commanders in Vietnam was escalating at an even faster pace. The war was costing blood and treasure, and Johnson's focus remained on winning a war that many considered unwinnable and unnecessary. In October 1967, after 300,000 rallied in Washington to protest the war, they moved to the Pentagon, where a violent confrontation with the military and police ensued.

Johnson's decision not to run in 1968 created a mess for the Democrats as the party splintered. Seeing an opportunity to run as the anti-Vietnam War candidate, Senator Eugene McCarthy of Minnesota entered the race. Senator Robert F. Kennedy from New York entered the race looking for young voters and those who longed for a return of "Camelot" to the White House under his brother. Kennedy and McCarthy were splitting the vote in the primaries when things abruptly changed. Kennedy was assassinated in California after delivering his victory speech in June 1968. This opened the door for Vice President Hubert H. Humphrey, known as the "happy warrior," to position himself as a more conservative Democrat. He criticized McCarthy as being an extremist with no plan to end the war.

In issues management, the social and political environment influence your success, The manager must be in toon with the external environment and trends to effectively position the issue and control the narrative. In the 1960s, both Democrats and Republicans were moving to the extremes. New coalitions were forming. New leaders were challenging the old guard. These dynamics are present within every organization. Issues serve to speed up the process of change and to establish a new equilibrium.

Richard Milhous Nixon was as unlikely as anyone to be the Republican nominee in 1968. Nixon had been Eisenhower's vice president for two terms. He ran for president to succeed Eisenhower in 1960 but lost to John F. Kennedy. After his loss, Nixon returned to his native California, where in 1962, he lost his race for governor to Pat Brown by 300,000 votes.

Most people thought that two major campaign losses over a period of only two years would end his political career. Nixon thought so himself saying after his loss for governor: "You (the press) won't have Nixon to kick around anymore." The reports of Nixon's political death were premature. He would resurrect himself politically by 1968. It would be the first of two improbable comebacks for Richard M. Nixon.

Historian Rick Perlstein summed up the 1968 election this way: "voters were angry at liberalism, angry at race riots in the city, and angry at violence on campuses." The political environment was primed to accept a change in direction. "In 1968, Richard Nixon handily mobilized law-and-order sentiment against urban disorder by pinning all the insurgencies, troubles and miseries on Democratic leadership," as reported in a retrospective in *USA Today*.

In issues management, extreme positions rarely have the advantage in the court of public opinion. This means that invectives and over-the-top proposals should be avoided. The public views issue management through the lens of problem/solution. Let the public know that you understand their concerns and offer a practical course of action in response.

In the campaign he promised to get us out of Vietnam. Nixon was old guard in terms of how he viewed American prestige and power. He believed that a hasty withdrawal was not a feasible option. The Office of the Historian wrote: "He knew that ending this war honorably was essential to his success in the presidency." He would work on achieving "peace with honor" from 1969 to 1973. Nixon was by no means the antiwar president.

There is a lesson here on timing in issues management, and it is that you can take all the time you need to resolve an issue as long as you stay on message and be perceived as on course toward a solution. Nixon's goal to get out of Vietnam had built-in flexibility and if his actions over that period all pointed in that direction, the public would stay with him.

Richard Nixon was a pragmatist. He did not govern as a conservative and many of his policies could be defined as liberal. He was not opposed to government intervention, mandates, or creating new programs when he thought they were needed. Nixon's first term began on January 20, 1969. He entered office with a 59 percent approval rating. It would peak at 67 percent in November and return to 59 percent in December of 1969.

Pragmatic domestically and skilled in foreign policy, Nixon was not a trusting man, and events were about to bring that into focus.

On June 13, 1971, *The New York Times* published what would become known as the "Pentagon Papers." These were an account of U.S. involvement in Vietnam from 1945 to 1967. The papers were provided by analyst for the Secretary of Defense, Daniel Ellsberg, a former Marine Corps officer, who "believed that the information contained in the Pentagon Papers about U.S. decision-making regarding Vietnam should be more widely available to the American public." The papers showed President Kennedy's involvement in the assassination of a Vietnam leader in 1963 and contradicted reports that the bombing, which was touted as destroying the North's willingness to wage war, had negligible impact on morale or war capability. The Supreme Court allowed their publication. Nixon saw the papers as embarrassing to the office of the presidency, and the actions of Ellsberg rekindled his mistrust of the press.

In 1972, Nixon had listening devices installed on telephones at Camp David (retreat in Maryland for the president,) and taping was installed to capture conversations in the White House. On June 17, 1972, a break-in at Democratic headquarters in the Watergate Hotel in Washington DC was foiled. Authorities confiscated listening devices and cash. On June 23rd, Nixon attempted to order the Federal Bureau of Investigation to stop looking into the events at Watergate. These were decisions that would come back to hurt the president over the next few years. At this point, President Nixon had chosen a course of action to ignore an issue that in the broader context of his presidency did not seem that important. He was wrong.

Building and maintaining trust with your team is one of the highest responsibilities for an issues management leader. There can be no alignment or cohesion without trust. If an issue becomes a crisis, then there is no time for second-guessing. In Nixon, we saw a leader who was measured in trusting others and as a result he would not receive trust in return.

On November 7, 1972, President Richard Nixon defeated far-left Senator George McGovern in one of the largest landslide victories in history. It was an explanation point placed on his 1968 victory. As chronicled: "McGovern came to symbolize a candidacy of radical children, rioters, marijuana smokers, draft dodgers, and hippies." In 1972, McGovern lost support from ethnic voters, blue-collar workers, and Southerners of all income levels shattering the Roosevelt coalition. He won only Massachusetts and the District of Columbia for a total of 17 electoral votes. Nixon had defused and defanged the antiwar movement, and the Democratic Party was slow to see this shift.

Again, the issues management lesson is effectively reading the environment. Democrats blamed their loss in 1968 on running a middle-of-the-road candidate, so they moved hard left. Nixon correctly calculated social change and positioned himself to benefit from this shift. Understanding the external environment is critical in issues management. A miscalculation will quickly position you as out of step, resulting in the loss of public support.

Nixon's second term would never fulfill its promise as his mistakes early on in Watergate and his innate distrust of people would come back to haunt him. Unlike presidents who had come before him, Nixon's colossal election victory was not a mandate from the voters, as much as it was a rejection of the Democratic candidate, so he did not have a mandate to change the trajectory of America.

Watergate was not an issue for Nixon at the beginning of his second term, but the wagons were beginning to circle. According to a timeline constructed by PBS, on August 1, 1972: "The Washington Post reported that a $25,000 check intended for Nixon's 1972 reelection campaign was deposited in the bank account of one of the Watergate burglars." *The Washington Post* would go on to report on October 10, 1972: "FBI had concluded the Watergate break-in was part of a broader spying effort connected to Nixon's campaign." The smoke was there; the only question is would it create a fire?

On January 13, 1973, more than six months after the break-in at Watergate, *The New York Times* reported: "At least four of the five men arrested last June in the Watergate raid are still being paid by persons as yet unnamed, according to sources close to the case." The article went on to cite:

High officials of the Committee for the Re-election of the President have acknowledged privately that they are unable to account for $900,000 in cash raised for President Nixon's 1972 campaign—far more than the $235,000 mentioned in court as the cost of the activities of the Watergate group.

They also reported: "One member of the Watergate team, Eugenio Rolando Martinez, was an active employee (sic) of the Central Intelligence Agency at the time of the break-in and kept a diary."

Hang a light on it is an adage of public relations when you are managing a potentially damaging issue. Facts are facts and misstating them is tantamount to lying. Nixon's dislike of the press caused him to underestimate its resolve and misjudge its power. In issues management the press is not your friend. It will print damaging stories and misinterpret the facts from time to time. This said there is no reason to go out of your way to make the press your enemy.

Over the next six months, the dominos would start to fall as the heat continued to rise on Nixon. In April 1973, Nixon's senior advisers, H.R. Haldeman and John Ehrlichman, resigned. Shortly thereafter, a special council, Archibald Cox, was appointed to investigate the entire matter of Watergate. Then, a witness at a Senate hearing revealed that Nixon secretly taped conversations in the White House. Nixon refused to release the tapes citing executive privilege.

On October 23, 1973, Nixon ordered his Attorney General, Eliot Richardson, to fire Archibald Cox. He refused and resigned. He then commanded his replacement, William Ruckelshaus, to fire Cox and he too refused and resigned. Robert Bork, serving as solicitor general, carried out Nixon's order and fired Cox. The events of that day became known as the "Saturday Night Massacre," which, in some ways, would mark the end of the Nixon presidency. He had lost trust in his authority to lead by operating outside the boundaries of his authority.

A *New York Times* tribute to William Ruckelshaus upon his death read:

The dismissals, all on Saturday, Oct. 20, labeled the "Saturday Night Massacre"' by news media, set off a firestorm of protest across the country. Some 300,000 telegrams inundated Congress and the White House, mostly calling for Nixon's resignation. The outcry was so ferocious that the White House said within days that it had decided to surrender the tape recordings.

A problem had grown into a crisis and the public was now paying attention. Nixon's power to govern was severely damaged by these events.

Cox would be reinstated by a federal judge. The tapes were made public. Nixon was on an unalterable course toward resignation or impeachment. On August 8, 1974, Nixon resigned. The reason the Saturday Night Massacre is so important is that it marks the point where an executive had lost his moral authority to lead. Nixon had broken many of the rules of issues management and would now pay the ultimate price for his failure.

Lessons

At Issue: Nixon allowed a problem to grow into a crisis.

Lesson: President Nixon teaches us that power and position do not immunize a leader from responsibility.

1. **No Plan:** Nixon took a defensive posture in managing Watergate. He reacted as new information became available rather than taking the initiative by creating a plan. In a crisis, you should never position yourself to swat away the balls as they are thrown at you. Crisis demands an active, forward-looking plan from the beginning. It cannot be managed piecemeal because it will take on a life of its own and become unmanageable.

2. **Snowball Effect:** As the crisis continued to grow, the public stopped assessing each event associated with the crisis on its merits. The result was Nixon had to shoulder the cumulative burden of all the issues that combined into a destructive narrative. He was crushed under the weight of a scandal that outgrew his ability to manage it.

3. **Ignoring It:** It is a mistake to believe that if they don't talk about an issue, it will go away. Watergate had too many moving parts, and too many of them led back to the White House, to believe it would go away. Never assume that no one will find out. Plan for the worst-case scenario and be happy when it does not happen.

4. **Misread Issue's Severity:** Consequences and fallout are not always obvious to the issue manager at the beginning. This is why creating a team is important whose members possess a variety of skills and who will speak truth to power. It is also important to understand the limits of your power and the protections it provides to you as the leader.

Nixon failed to grasp that even the presidency could not protect him from the fallout over Watergate.

5. **Failure to Prioritize Issues**: A common mistake in issues management is not ordering priorities correctly. Each issue has a different level of risk and reward associated with it, and fallout varies at various levels within an organization. In the beginning, Watergate was a dirty trick played out in the context of a political campaign, but in the end, it became a presidential cover-up and an impeachable offense. Every issue is important at some level and to someone. The more touch points the issue has within your organization, the more potential exposure you have while managing it. Nixon should have understood, or been told, that this issue reached into his inner circle. The internal assessment and warning structure failed.

6. **Underestimated the Press**: Nixon did not like or trust the press, neither of which are important in issues management. Bob Woodward and Carl Bernstein at *The Washington Post* doggedly pursued every lead until a second-rate burglary became a first-rate scandal. At first the Post was alone in its reporting of Watergate, but as they found more connections to the White House, it became a story reported nationally. That is how the media works. The lesson here is the press has a job to do which sometimes includes presenting the other side of your narrative. When the press is out for a story give them a story from your point of view and accept that this is the best you can do at the time.

7. **Support**: Nixon was not beloved like FDR or John Kennedy. He was not a war hero like Eisenhower. He was a capable issues manager as president but was not associated with a movement or a cause. Therefore, he had no natural constituency. This hurt him when the scandal hit because there was no one to break his fall. In issues management, enemies are the known-known, but not having good friends is the unknown-unknown because it is difficult to predict how they will react.

8. **Goodwill**: Nixon's response to the evolving crisis was to say,: "I am not a crook." He would go on to state when Congress investigated his finances: "I have earned every cent. And in all of my years in public life I have never obstructed justice." Nixon's laments were ignored as most of the damage had already been done. When you are

perceived as losing there is nothing to break your fall and forgiveness is in short supply. Reputation is a very fragile commodity and once lost it is exceedingly difficult to regain.

9. **Stepping Up**: All blame flows to the top. It was the president's men who hatched the scheme to burglarize Watergate, and it should have been his men who stepped in early and stopped the bleeding. They did not. The issues manager needs to build into the team that we are all in this together and that every member has a responsibility to the team and the organization. Leaders and their teams need to own mistakes—not ignore them.

10. **Brushfires**: Besides denying he was personally involved; Nixon never undertook a public relations program to recast or reframe Watergate as Kennedy did after the Bay of Pigs. The lesson here is that when faced with unfavorable, or even lethal issues, you need to act strategically and decisively. Nixon early on could have created a narrative that put the burglary into a perspective that minimized its potential to damage his presidency. He eventually fell on his sword, but it was too late. He mixed up defense with offense in trying to stop investigations and limit access to information. In 21 months, Nixon's landslide victory was turned into public humiliation as he was forced to resign.

11. **Alignment**: Nixon lost his key advisors and was left with few resources available to him. Nixon held the most powerful job in the world, but in the end, it was just Richard Nixon versus the law. His power to control events and remain the leader of our government had been stripped away by a series of missteps. The lesson here is never assume that power and resources will always be there for you.

Nixon lost much of his authority to govern after the "Saturday Night Massacre." Symbolically it was the end of Nixon's presidency. After that day in October 1973, Nixon's enemies would go after his taxes and force him to pay back taxes. His circle of friends shriveled as his power ebbed and his influence faded. A mismanaged issue had destroyed his presidency. He resigned in August 1974. This is a classic lose-lose outcome.

Richard Nixon had nine lives. Losing two elections in 1960 and 1962 did not end his political career, and his resignation would not end Nixon's career in public life either. In the years following his presidency, Nixon wrote his memoirs and nine other books. He visited many foreign nations as an elder statesman and was viewed as an expert on foreign affairs. He rehabilitated his public image before his passing in 1994. There is a valuable lesson to be learned from Nixon here too. Crisis changes things and may even change people, but there are always new opportunities available to pursue. America is the land of second chances. Richard Nixon proved that to be true.

Now let's turn to the presidency of Gerald R. Ford, who, like Truman, was forced by events to make a big decision right out of the gate.

CHAPTER 8

Ford—Getting Ahead of the Public

Restating the words from Martin Luther King Jr. provides a valuable lesson in issues management for this chapter: "A genuine leader is not a searcher for consensus but a molder of consensus." A leader cannot get too far out in front of his stakeholders. They need to be brought along and prepared for the actions taken. Gerald R. Ford did the right thing for the nation in pardoning Richard Nixon, but he failed as an issue manager to mold consensus before making his decision.

Gerald R. Ford of Michigan was America's first unelected president. He assumed office upon the resignation of Richard Nixon on August 9, 1974. The 25th amendment was passed by Congress on July 6, 1965 and was ratified by the states on February 10, 1967. The amendment was in response to the assassination of John F. Kennedy. Had the gunshot wound not killed him but left him incapacitated, he would still have been president under the constitution as written at that time. The new amendment dealt with four eventualities: death, removal, resignation, or incapacitation.

The fact is during the time that Lyndon Johnson served out the remainder of John F. Kennedy's first term (November 22, 1963 to January 20, 1965), the United States did not have a vice president. Had Johnson died in office during that time, the powers of the presidency would have gone to the speaker of the House of Representatives.

Under the new amendment, Gerald Ford was appointed vice president upon the resignation of Vice President Spiro Agnew, who was elected as Nixon's vice president and then involved in a scandal and forced to resign. Ford had served as minority leader in the House of Representatives since 1965 and had been a member of Congress since 1949, representing the fifth district of Michigan.

Upon being sworn in as president, Ford said:

I have not sought this enormous responsibility, but I will not
shirk it . . . I believe that truth is the glue that holds government
together, not only our Government (sic), but civilization itself.
That bond, though strained, is unbroken at home and abroad. In
all my public and private acts as your President, I expect to follow my instincts of openness and candor with full confidence that
honesty is always the best policy in the end. My fellow Americans,
our long national nightmare is over. Our Constitution works; our
great Republic is a Government (sic) of laws and not of men. Here
the people rule.

Ford would follow his instincts and ignore an important rule of issues
management—bring the public with you on important decisions.

As an appointed president, Gerald R. Ford did not have the benefits
derived from coming to office after having competed in primary elections
to win the endorsement of his party: being nominated at his party's convention; giving an acceptance speech where he would outline his vision
for America; running a general election campaign against a Democratic
opponent; winning the majority of electoral votes; giving a victory speech
on election night; taking the oath of office before a cheering crowd on
January 20th; reveling in the playing of "Hail to the Chief" in his honor
for the first time, and delivering his inaugural address. Rather, Gerald
Ford was replacing a disgraced president, who had selected him to replace
his dishonored vice president under the terms of an amendment to the
constitution that was being used for the first time in history.

In issues management, as we saw with Franklin Roosevelt, asking
permission and obtaining a mandate are especially important to creating
a solid foundation for success in carrying out your programs. Ford, as
an issues manager, did not have these benefits, and it would cost him in
the end.

According to Gallup polling conducted the week after Richard Nixon
left office, Ford enjoyed a 71 percent approval rating which was behind
only Truman at 87 percent in 1945 and Johnson at 78 percent in early

1964. Ironically, both men had assumed the office of president also under extraordinary circumstances. Unlike his two predecessors, in Ford's case, Americans were ready to move on from Nixon.

In his address to Congress on August 12, 1974, Ford clearly stated that he would not follow Lyndon Johnson's lead in expanding government: "A government big enough to give you everything you want is a government big enough to take from you everything you have." He would also tell Congress: "I do not want a honeymoon with you. I want a good marriage."

Ford was shaped by his career in Congress and had profound respect for the institutions of government and its processes. He told Congress that he would focus on taming inflation. In 1965, the Consumer Price Index stood at 31.5 and was increasing at 1.6 percent. In 1974, the index was 49.3 and was increasing at a rate of 11.4 percent. The reason for the growth in inflation was the rising costs of food and energy prices and the lifting of Nixon's wage-price controls. Also, federal spending had exploded during the Johnson and Nixon years. In 1964, Kennedy's last budget, federal outlays were $118 billion. By 1975, Nixon's last budget, they had grown to $332 billion.

Ford's program was named Whip Inflation Now (WIN) and asked Americans to save more of their money. Ford found himself caught between trying to lower inflation and at the same time dealing with rising unemployment. By the time Ford left office in 1977, the CPI stood at 60.6 and was increasing at a rate of 6.5 percent per year.

As an issues manager out of the gate, Ford was in step with the American people. He was addressing the most prominent issue and seemed to have a strategy to defeat inflation. The public did not expect the Vietnam War to end the next day because Nixon promised to end it, but as long as he stayed the course, then he would have public support. The same could be applied to Ford. He had a plan, and the public gave him the benefit of the doubt.

Ford's second move happened on August 20, 1974. On that day, he nominated Nelson Rockefeller of New York to be his vice president. Rockefeller had been governor of New York from 1959 until 1973, when he stepped down. He was a northeastern Republican who supported larger state government by spending more on education, environmental protection, transportation, housing, welfare, medical aid, civil rights, and the arts. Rockefeller had sought his party's nomination for president in 1960, 1964, and 1968. The nomination of Rockefeller signaled that Ford intended to govern as a moderate rather than as a conservative— a movement within the Republican Party that was gaining momentum. This immediately created suspicion about Ford on his right flank.

In issues management big decisions send signals. This is particularly true with personnel decisions. You need to be careful when selecting your top lieutenants because a leader is often defined by those choices.

The third big move Ford made early in his presidency was on September 8, 1974, when he pardoned Richard Nixon for any crimes he may have committed while president. The next day, *The New York Times* reported on Ford's rationale for the pardon by printing his remarks at his press briefing, "the tranquility (sic) to which this nation has been restored by the events of recent weeks could be irreparably lost." Ford believed that there would be nothing to gain from indicting a former president or from other actions that would continue to resurrect the pain caused by the scandal known as Watergate. The article also quoted Tom DeFrank, a *Newsweek* reporter, who was in the briefing room when Ford made the announcement as saying: "No one could believe it." The American people certainly were not ready for this action. Gallup polling reported:

> Ford's job approval rating plummeted to 50 percent in late September 1974, after he pardoned Nixon. By January 1975, his approval rating had fallen below 40 percent, and it remained at that level until April 1975. His lowest approval rating would be 37 percent between January and March 1975.

There are two lessons here in issues management: First, issues need context to be understood, and second, assessment of the gravity of his decision was inadequate. He provided only an incomplete rationale for his action which was abrupt and appeared not well thought out. He did not build a foundation of support around his decision before acting or a communication plan to explain the action to the public. As a result, Ford put no cushion between himself and the public response to his action and opened the door for rumor and inuendo to shape the narrative. Ford's leverage to govern, trust and reservoir of goodwill were immediately depleted as a result.

In this environment he delivered his first State of the Union address on January 15, 1975, Ford told the American people:

> I must say to you that the state of the Union is not good: Millions of Americans are out of work. Recession and inflation are eroding the money of millions more. Prices are too high, and sales are too slow. This year's Federal deficit will be about $30 billion; next year's probably $45 billion. The national debt will rise to over $500 billion. Our plant capacity and productivity are not increasing fast enough. We depend on others for essential energy. Some people question their Government's ability to make hard decisions and stick with them; they expect Washington politics as usual.

Not an optimistic assessment and another unforced error by Ford right out of the gate.

As the remedy, Ford now called for tax cuts and restraining government spending by tying increases in government programs to no more than the rate of inflation. He also addressed energy listing three goals:

> First, we must reduce oil imports by 1 million barrels per day by the end of this year and by 2 million barrels per day by the end of 1977.
> Second, we must end vulnerability to economic disruption by foreign suppliers of oil by 1985.
> Third, we must develop our energy technology and resources so that the United States has the ability to supply a significant share of the energy needs of the free world by the end of this century.

In issues management, your stock as a leader is either rising or falling at any point in time. Ford had lost some political support from conservatives by nominating Rockefeller and lost a measure of trust from the American people with his pardon of Richard Nixon. Decisions have consequences, and your rationale for an action taken, however virtuous and noble, may not be appreciated by the public if you do not assume control of the narrative.

Ford ended his address by saying:

> As our 200th anniversary approaches (1976), we owe it to ourselves and to posterity to rebuild our political and economic strength. Let us make America once again and for centuries more to come what it has so long been—a stronghold and a beacon-light of liberty for the whole world.

Ford would welcome in America's bicentennial on July 4, 1976, and welcome HRH Elizabeth to America on July 7, 1976.

Ford governed domestically as a moderate. In foreign policy, the White House wrote: "Ford acted vigorously to maintain U.S. power and prestige." He kept an eye on Southeast Asia, worked to prevent new wars in the Middle East, pursued the continuance of detente with the Soviet Union, and sought limitations on nuclear weapons stockpiles.

Ford in some ways was like a captain of a ship who adjusted course after a storm. His main mission, as he said it, was to heal the nation and restore a sense of normalcy after the events of the past decade. By 1976, he could claim: "Reduction in the rate of inflation is expected to coincide with a healthy recovery in the standard of living." And the world was at peace. Could Ford overcome the image as a placeholder president and the political and public relations problems he created early in his presidency? According to Gallup, "Ford began the election year of 1976 with a 46 percent approval rating, an ominous sign for a sitting president seeking re-election."

In issues management, allowing early mistakes to linger can create challenges to your leadership. In Ford's case, this meant he would be challenged for the nomination by Ronald Reagan who was now the leader of the conservative wing of the Republican Party. Reagan had legitimacy to mount a challenge because Ford was never elected president, and he had support because Ford had turned his back on the conservative wing of the party with his nomination of Rockefeller.

Stephen Hess reported:

> If I remember correctly, the president, Gerald Ford, was winning, winning, winning from New Hampshire on, and then suddenly

he hit a block in North Carolina and Gov. Reagan started to win, win, win. So suddenly they came into the convention almost tied.

Reagan did not win the nomination, but he clearly positioned himself as the heir apparent in 1980 were Ford to lose the election.

In the general election, Ford was challenged by Democrat James Earl Carter of Georgia. He would lose by about 1.5 million total votes and 57 electoral votes. Republican enthusiasm was with its conservative wing. America was ready to close the book on a turbulent decade that saw riots on our streets, protests on our campuses, a war we could not win, one president choosing not to run and another who disgraced his office and resigned, burgeoning government spending and debt, high inflation, and a state of our union that a president described as "not good." A good and decent man, who served as a placeholder in history, would pay the last debt to a turbulent decade.

There are times when those who succeed a leader not only inherit the issues left unresolved but also ultimately pay the price for the failures of his predecessor in issues management. If you ascend to leadership, then one of your first jobs is to scan the field to understand the failings and miscalculations you have inherited from your predecessor and address them right out of the gate.

Gerald Ford would serve as president for about 30 months. In his remarks after his swearing-in, Ford said:

I feel it is my first duty to make an unprecedented compact with my countrymen. Not an inaugural address, not a fireside chat, not a campaign speech—just a little straight talk among friends. And I intend it to be the first of many.

He acknowledged: "I am acutely aware that you have not elected me as your President."

Ford created a clear launch point for his presidency: "My fellow Americans, our long national nightmare is over. Our Constitution works; our great Republic is a government of laws and not of men." And he asked the American people to forgive and move on: "I ask again your prayers, for Richard Nixon and for his family." The trouble for Ford was that it was not as simple as it sounded. Issues management is a process in which support and understanding need to be in place before action is taken. When you miss steps in the process, you pay a price.

Ford made the right first move in focusing on inflation, but his next two moves derailed his momentum, created enemies, and altered the trust people had in him as a leader.

Lessons

At Issue: Ford pardons Nixon short-circuiting the forgiveness process and squandering goodwill.

Lesson: President Ford provides a lesson on the importance of the right first move. He made three important decisions early in his presidency, and two of them created new issues that were problems for him during his entire term in office.

1. **First Moves**: Ford addressed inflation that was hurting the nation but also appointed Rockefeller as vice president and pardoned Richard Nixon. The Rockefeller choice distanced him from conservatives, and the pardon lowered public support. In issues management, the most important thing is to succeed early. Focus like a laser on actions that produce positive results quickly.

2. **Timing**: Healing happens at its own pace. Watergate was a traumatic event in our history. In issues management, it is not the job of the leader to tell a community that it is time to move on and put the issue behind them. Let the community tell you when it is time to move on. Again, the need to listen cannot be overstated when managing an issue.

3. **Run Its Course**: Solving a problem because you have a solution ready is not always the best choice. The pardon issue was not yet ripe when Ford acted. The action was premature. The public had not yet reconciled what had happened under Nixon. Ford's goal of moving on did not synchronize with where the public was at that moment. In issues management, Watergate was Nixon's problem to own, and he was the one who had to do what was needed to regain trust and attain forgiveness. Ford short circuited the process. He would have been better served to let the process run its course.

4. **Context**: The pardon of Nixon came unexpectedly. Ford, as an issues manager, did not create context from which the pardon would be the understandable outcome. He would have benefited from proposing a series of reforms that would stop another Watergate from happening. In issues management, it is good practice to make sure that your audience understands why an action is taken by providing a sound rationale to generate support and understanding in advance of action. Intention and action should intersect in issues management. Intention (purpose) must always be clear and tied to outcomes and results. Remember, the focus of issues management is finding a resolution to the conflict.

5. **Mandate**: Ford never had a mandate to act because he was not elected. In issues management, it is important to honestly assess your power to act. Ford was a transitional figure who was president only because of the 25th amendment. He needed early successes to build on more than most. In issues management, you never want to exceed your mandate, and you need to develop a high level of trust when you do not have a mandate.

6. **Leadership**: Leadership is not always rewarded. In issues management, doing the right thing before doing the little things to support your decision can create new issues. Leadership is measured by action, but it must be the right action that brings key stakeholders along with you. Going off script or getting too far ahead of the public runs the risk of losing control of the issue.

7. **Opening the Door**: Ford split his party by nominating Rockefeller and lost support for pardoning Nixon. As a result, he opened the door for a primary challenge from a conservative candidate in 1980 after less than a month in office. One of the tricky parts of issues management is measuring the consequences of action in advance. You do not want to provide a rationale to justify team members abandoning the plan or challenges from within. You also do not want to do things that distract the public from what you are trying to accomplish. That is why it is imperative that as a leader you endeavor to create broad understanding and support for your actions so that coalitions do not fracture.

8. **Blame and Responsibility**: In issues management you accept responsibility, and try to avoid blame. This is often a fine line to walk.

Ford, by interjecting himself into Watergate, disrupted this balance. He needed a measurable victory before even thinking about a pardon. He needed to build his political capital and not relive the past. Victories underpin success. Success builds momentum. Momentum puts you in control of the narrative.

9. **Paying the Price**: Life is not fair. Nixon resigned, returned home to California, and was pardoned. Ford was left to clean up the mess. Reagan would challenge him in the primary, and Carter would defeat him in the general election. In issues management, there are times when, unfairly, you will find yourself in the position of having to pay a debt you do not owe. Ford created this issue for himself.

10. **Original Sin**: There is a tipping point in the management of every issue that is determined by the actions you take and to a lesser degree by factors you cannot control. President Gerald R. Ford chose the wrong first moves, and in doing so, he created a public environment where the American people were ready to move on from two decades of turmoil and disruption.

Gerald Ford was handed a fractured nation. His instinct was to move quickly and put it behind him. This is not the way issues management works. A manager is not graded on the speed of action or the decisiveness in which he executes, but rather on the effectiveness of the action measured by how well it positions him to move forward to accomplish other goals and build momentum. The pardon stalled Ford's presidency.

Ford failed to fully appreciate the environment in which this most weighty decision of his presidency was made, and instead chose to focus the public on the outcome he desired to heal the nation.

Next up is Jimmy Carter as America turns the page.

CHAPTER 9

Carter—Losing Focus

In his book, *The Mamba Mentality*, the late basketball great Kobe Bryant wrote: "A lot of leaders fail because they don't have the bravery to touch that nerve or strike that chord." Jimmy Carter was brave and a man of strong convictions, but these qualities may have been too strong in a role that requires compromise. Leaders must possess flexibility. This is not an abandonment of beliefs and convictions but rather a concession to practicality. Issues management is not about absolutes. Rather, it is more about the art of the possible. Carter's strict moral compass provided him with strength and determination but also proved to be a challenge when he operated in gray areas as an issues manager.

Carter was elected governor of Georgia in 1970 after losing in 1966. Miller Center writes: "The new governor's inaugural address surprised many Georgians by calling for an end to segregation and received national attention for it." As governor, "[H]is primary concern was the state's outdated, wasteful government bureaucracy. Three hundred state agencies were channeled into two dozen 'superagencies.' He promoted environmental protection and greater funding for the schools." He had a reputation of being arrogant, aloof, and holier than thou as governor.

Upon his announcement for president, *The New York Times* reported: "Jimmy Carter, the moderate Georgia Governor who is regarded by supporters as a Southern-style Kennedy and by skeptics as just another Democratic dark horse, announced his candidacy for President tonight." The reporting goes on to write:

> One factor in his favor is his service as chairman of the party's committee that coordinated the 1974 congressional and gubernatorial campaigns—a job that brought him into close contact with almost every major Democratic candidate and gave him a reputation as a tactician and organizer.

Carter faced two liberals in the primaries, defeating both Morris Udall of Arizona and Jerry Brown of California. He was then free to position himself as a reformer and as a Washington outsider in his race against Gerald Ford, who would become the first incumbent president to lose since Herbert Hoover in 1932.

The issues management lesson here is how quickly the environment shifts and how important it is to understand these shifts and position within them. Carter was an outsider in a time when America was looking to turn the page. The same would be true in 2008, when a junior senator from Illinois, Barack Obama, jumped into the race for president with little experience and few accomplishments because the time was right. Timing is everything.

Carter's victory in 1976 put an exclamation point on Ford's missed opportunity to institute broad ethics and campaign reforms in the wake of Watergate. These reforms would have made him less vulnerable when running against a reformer and outsider. Also, Ford would lose New York state (Rockefeller was off the ticket and replaced by Bob Dole), which showed that Ford's decision to make the former governor his vice president paid few dividends. In fact, Rockefeller was attempting to use his state's delegation against him at the nominating convention.

According to the White House:

> Jimmy Carter aspired to make Government "competent and compassionate," responsive to the American people and their expectations. His achievements were laudable, but in an era of rising energy costs, mounting inflation, and continuing global tensions, it would be difficult for his administration to meet these high expectations.

Again, the environment often provides the parameters in which you can operate as an issues manager. At times it is green-lighting bold action, and at other times, it limits your ability to act. This is why understanding the environment in which an issue is managed is especially important.

Carter was both an engineer, who prided himself on making systems work better and run more efficiently, and an idealist who possessed a near uncompromising sense of morality and right and wrong. These attributes were earned as a mathematics major in college, a nuclear submariner in the navy, and his strong faith and adherence to Christian religious principles. He was now about to be challenged in applying these skills and beliefs to a weak economy and an increasingly hostile world.

Like Ford, Carter's first act as president was one of compassion. He pardoned those who dodged the draft for the Vietnam War. Carter was closing the door on Vietnam and the social unrest that grew because of it. In a way that was his electoral mandate. It is ironic how the two pardons (Nixon and draft dodgers) could have such different outcomes. Read the room!

As advertised, Carter was a reformer as he "introduced and got passed the Ethics in Government Act that first protected whistle-blowers." He also established the Foreign Intelligence Surveillance Act in 1978 (FISA) and Federal Emergency Management Agency (FEMA) in 1979 and conducted emergency planning. This, in a way, closed the door on Watergate, something Ford was never able to do.

In issues management, look for doors that have been left open and have some remaining problems to solve because there is an advantage to closing them by achieving early successes. Study the people who proceeded you to examine their successes, failures, and, most importantly, the things they left incomplete.

True to his principles, in foreign policy, Carter would bring Israel and Egypt together to sign the Camp David Accords. He would establish full diplomatic relations with China. Carter signed the Panama Canal Treaty that set in motion the canal's return to Panama by the year 2000 and guaranteed its neutrality. And Carter would shift focus to human rights. Some argue that this focus gave impetus to the ending of the USSR and communist expansion without war being waged.

Carter was a man of strong convictions, and it came through in the way he viewed the issues he managed:

1. **Energy**: He demanded conservation and framed the issues as the "moral equivalent of war." The price of gasoline was $0.61 in 1976 and would rise to $1.25 by 1980. The American people experienced shortages in gas lines, and most were never convinced they were fighting a moral war.

2. **Communism**: This was an enemy every president had fought since Winston Churchill defined USSR expansion as an "Iron Curtain" after World War II. Carter believed the focus should shift to human rights. In his commencement speech at Notre Dame on May 22, 1977, he said: "We can no longer separate the traditional issues of war and peace from the new global questions of justice, equity, and human rights." His policy shift would play a role in Carter boycotting the 1980 Olympic games in Moscow, citing human rights abuses by USSR in Afghanistan.

Carter's skills set was an interesting mix that combined engineering with idealism. These two parts of him would shape his policies regarding Russia, China, the Middle East, poor nations, the military, domestic policy, energy, and the economy. By 1979, he would have the lowest approval rating of any president in three decades. A review of some of his speeches provides some insight into Carter's beliefs:

1. **Energy Speech 1977**: He chastised the American people: "Our biggest problem, however, is that we simply use too much and waste too much energy ... Although all countries could, of course, be more efficient, we are the worst offender."
2. **State of the Union 1978**: He blamed the American lifestyle for the problems: "Every day we spend more than $120 million for foreign oil." He then went on to prescribe his three R's: "Reconciliation of private needs and interests into a higher purpose. Rebuilding the old dreams of justice and liberty, and country and community. Rebirth of our faith in the common good."
3. **Crisis of Confidence 1979**: In this talk, he indicted his own leadership: "Our people are losing that faith, not only in government itself but in the ability as citizens to serve as the ultimate rulers and shapers of our democracy." This would be referred to as his "malaise speech" by Senator Edward Kennedy.

Carter, at times, imposed his values on the American people rather than building support around his goals. This is one reason why he lost support quickly when he did not produce results in managing issues.

Buying in is very important in building a bigger and welcoming tent in support of an agenda or strategy. His approach also emboldened opposition, like in the case of Gerald Ford, and he would be challenged for his party's nomination in 1980.

Carter was a centrist who did not possess the charisma, support, mandate, or political abilities to move his party to the center. Liberals wanted an activist government to fix the economy. Carter was not that kind of Democrat.

Carter's goal of making government more efficient, thereby lowering its costs, was compounded by the fact that many "Great Society" programs, including Medicare and Medicaid, grew organically. In 1978, Carter's first budget, federal expenditures were $457 billion and by 1981, his last budget, they had risen to $678 billion. Carter would discover that neither efficiency nor sacrifice were enough to curb federal spending.

On June 9, 1979, *The New York Times* reported on the results of a poll that they stated found "overall approval of Mr. Carter's handling of the Presidency dropped from 42 percent in March to 30 percent this month, lower than the worst rating of any recent President except Richard M. Nixon or Harry S. Truman." The reporting went on to point out what I will call "Carter's Dilemma" writing: "Mr. Carter ... appeared to have the politically unfortunate knack of generating personal opposition from those who disagreed with him, on issues like strategic arms, without getting enhanced backing from those who agreed with him." He did not build support as he moved his agenda forward.

Effective issues management has a goal of addition, not subtraction. You want to create a strategy and use tactics that bring more people to support your positions rather than lose support especially within your base. Carter either lacked this ability or was so convinced of the correctness of his positions that he often drove people away. Like Nixon before him, when things got bad for Carter, there were very few people who had his back. With a bad economy, sinking poll numbers, and opposition growing within his own party, Carter would now face his greatest challenge—Americans taken hostage in Iran.

Iran is a Persian, Shite-Islamic nation in the Middle East. For much of its modern history, it has been a monarchy ruled by an emperor. Modern-day Iran was "created" by the Tehran Declaration during World

War II. Postwar, Iran was ruled by Mohammad Reza Shah Pahlavi, who considered creating a constitutional republic form of government. "The Shah," as he was known, was closely aligned with the west.

Like in Cuba and Vietnam, Iran was a country that dealt with several foreign interventions. Its resources were being plundered and its culture was being lost. As in Cuba and Vietnam, an insurgency grew, focused on nationalism and getting rid of corruption. This resulted in internal strife. In Iran, the conflict was between the pro-western ruling class, who controlled the country's oil wealth, and Islamic religious groups supporting national identity and culture. Theocrats would purge the Shah from power, much like U.S. backed governments in Cuba and Vietnam, and he fled the nation.

On February 1, 1979, religious leader, Ayatollah Khomeini, returned to Iran and assumed ultimate power. This fledgling theocracy was antithetical to America, where government establishment of a national religion was constitutionally prohibited. Now, as an Islamic republic, religion would be at the core of all Iranian society.

One fallout of the revolution was the United States was now considered as an enemy of the new republic, often referred to as the "great Satan," resulting in many anti-U.S. demonstrations in Iran. These protests continued to escalate as reported by the State Department:

> On November 4, 1979, Iranian students seized the embassy and detained more than 50 Americans, ranging from the Chargé d'Affaires to the most junior members of the staff, as hostages. The Iranians held the American diplomats hostage for 444 days.

This would become known as the Iranian Hostage Crisis.

President Carter had three options: impose sanctions on Iran, execute a retaliatory military strike against Iran, or follow the path of diplomacy. The central question was which strategy had the best chance of saving the hostages' lives. Carter would issue Executive Orders 12170, 12172, and 12205, which froze Iran's assets, restricted immigration, and prohibited trade with Iran of items other than medical, including arms. That last order would set the stage for another crisis involving Carter's successor.

As his active strategy, Carter chose to negotiate, but his government was flying blind. The White House wrote:

> Gary Sick, who was on the National Security staff, recalled a meeting in which Vice President Walter Mondale asked the Central Intelligence Agency director Stansfield Turner, "What the hell is an 'Ayatollah' anyway." Turner said he wasn't sure he knew.

Carter had truly little intelligence on which to make decisions, and our CIA and State Department were at a loss to figure out exactly what a theocratic republic was and what it wanted from us. The demands soon became clear: Return the Shah to Iran in exchange for the American hostages.

Just like the Vietnam War, the Iranian Hostage Crisis was broadcast into America's homes every night. Roone Arledge, who headed ABC News at that time, created a new nighttime television news program just to chronicle the Iranian Hostage Crisis. It was called *Nightline* and was hosted by veteran journalist Ted Koppel.

Here we see two challenges frequently faced in issues management. The first is not having a reliable party with whom to negotiate in good faith, and the second is external factors speeding up the timeline putting unnecessary pressure on implementing a measured course of action. The media was shaping public opinion by counting each day the hostages were held and driving Americans to demand quick results. This forced Carter's hand.

Carter pursued negotiations for months, then he acted:

> Carter approved a hostage rescue mission by an elite paramilitary unit, the American commandos led by Colonel Charles Beckwith. It was a dismal failure. Several military helicopters broke down in the desert, and eight commandos died when two aircraft collided during the hasty retreat. The aborted mission seemed to many Americans a symbol of U.S. military weaknesses in the post-Vietnam era. Carter's popularity plunged to 20 percent, even lower than Nixon's during the Watergate.

In the view of the public, Carter had now failed domestically by not taming stagflation, militarily by the unsuccessful hostage rescue mission, and politically by damaging the image and prestige of America globally. The 1980 election loomed.

Not getting results exacerbates any negative perceptions that already exist. Issues management is more a try-and-succeed undertaking than it is a try-and-fail. The public sees the term "try" in different ways depending on the outcome. Carter needed to make the right move and he did not. Diplomacy had failed, and now the military mission option failed. He had painted himself into a corner and was running out of options.

Failure breeds challenges to your authority by emboldening your enemies. Carter was challenged by the most prominent liberal politician at the time, Senator Edward (Ted) Kennedy of Massachusetts, who was the youngest brother of former president John F. Kennedy. The fight between Carter and Kennedy would go all the way to the convention, where Kennedy finally conceded. Carter secured the nomination and faced Governor Ronald Reagan of California who was the leader of the conservative movement within the Republican Party. Carter refused to join in the first debate. He ran a limited campaign staying at the White House focused on bringing the hostages home. It was called his "rose garden strategy." Carter's only course of action was to wait. He had not only lost control of the narrative but also was no longer in charge of the issue.

Stu Eizenstat, one of Carter's top aides, would write in his book, *President Carter: The White House Years.* "It (Rose Garden Strategy) totally personalized the crisis in the American media by focusing the responsibility on the Oval Office and showing the terrorists they could put the American presidency itself into dysfunction." Carter's approval went through the floor. He lost his bid for reelection.

Lessons

At Issue: Jimmy Carter's presidency was crippled when Iranian revolutionaries took American diplomats hostage and held them in captivity for 444 days.

Lesson: President Carter teaches us about losing control of the issue after tactics fail to produce success.

1. **Issue in Control**: Carter lost control of the hostage issue when he ran out of viable options and ceded control of the issue to the hostage takers. In issues management, success builds momentum, and failure destroys it. Carter initially viewed the hostage crises through the lens of diplomacy, but he was negotiating with a mob. This left him with only a military response. You sometimes face asymmetrical issues that do not respond to a traditional approach. These are by far the most difficult and require more planning and expanded buy-ins before making your first move.

2. **Amplified Failure**: Going into the hostage crisis, Carter had low approval because of the economy. He went all-in managing the hostage crisis, which only served to magnify the public perception that he was a weak and ineffectual issues manager. This served to amplify failure. In issues management, failure often necessitates change. When you have failed in one area and left a mess, you cannot simply move on to the next area without having built substantial support. It is important in choosing your leader that the person has a record of success to build on and will be given the benefit of the doubt when things do not go as planned. You can't build on a foundation of failure.

3. **Proportionality**: Every issue has its place in the hierarchy of things you need to address. The question is how much time, effort, goodwill, and resources the issue deserves. Putting the Iran hostage crisis into an issues management perspective, Carter bet his presidency on solving it. Much like Johnson bet his presidency on winning the Vietnam War. There is no debate that it was a crisis, but was it a crisis that demanded the president's full attention when his only option was to wait for the other side to make a move? Inactivity may be warranted at times, but not when everyone knows that you have run out of options.

4. **Know Your Opponent**: President Carter was negotiating with "student revolutionaries" who had been part of a revolution that turned

Iran into a theocracy. Carter took a standard diplomatic approach to managing the crisis. His government did not fully comprehend what Iran had become or who was the ultimate decision-maker in the process. Therefore, his negotiations had little chance of success. In issues management, one of the corollaries to properly framing the issue is making sure that you are addressing the right decision-maker and audience. Negotiating with someone who does not have the power to execute or approve conditions is not productive, and selling your solution to the wrong audience does not advance the ball.

5. **Bright Light**: Carter elevated the hostage takers status by becoming personally involved in the crisis. Yes, the hostage takers held the cards because they had control over the lives of 66 Americans, but by shining such a bright light on the issue, Carter provided incentives to the hostage takers to keep the crisis going. They were at the center of the world stage, selling their revolution and getting free publicity every night on the news. Plus, they were exacting a form of punishment on the leader of a heretic nation they considered to be an enemy. In issues management, it is important to avoid making your issue a platform and a megaphone for an external stakeholder who does not have your best interests at heart.

6. **Sisyphus**: Carter managed a lot of issues, no different from any other president, but he had few victories. The hostage crisis served only to affirm the belief, held by many Americans, that Carter was not up to the demands of the job. In issues management, you first must be perceived as the person who is able to achieve results. The vibe from the Carter Administration was that he worked hard, methodically pushing the rock up the hill every day, but he never saw the sunrise over the summit.

7. **Playing a Bad Hand**: In issues management, it is good practice to check your chips before putting them on the table. Do not bet a $100 chip on a $10 hand. In Iran, Carter bet the prestige of the United States on a hand that he was not likely to win because he was not in control of the situation. He had assets of different values and he bet the ranch on a bad hand.

8. **Optics Matter**: The "Rose Garden Strategy" did not send the message that Carter was on the job and in control as he intended. Rather,

the optics showed a U.S. president reduced to waiting for student protesters to talk to him. He came off not only as powerless but also as optionless. In issues management, the sequencing of activities does not always go perfectly in terms of having negotiations move toward a conclusion, but the perception that they are moving to a conclusion cannot be overstated. In Carter's case, he was placing calls, and no one was picking up the telephone on the other end of the line. You always need a Plan B. Carter did not adjust quickly enough and ran out of options to resolve the issue as the clock ticked closer to election day.

9. **Force Failed**: The raid to free the hostages was a disaster. The equipment did not function properly. When managing issues, you always must grasp the extent of your power as an organization. You don't want to promise things that you cannot deliver or attempt things that have a high probability of ending in failure. The military mission could have succeeded, but was the price of failure too high to attempt it? By failing, Carter surrendered more of his leverage to the hostage takers and lost more political capital as the failure was hard to defend.

10. **Running on Empty**: In issues management you never want to run out of options. Carter had a military and a diplomatic option at the start. How he used diplomacy can be questioned because it elevated the status and provided a propaganda platform to the hostage takers. The military option he chose failed. It created a "lose-lose" for Carter by wasting opportunities, Note, Israel was able to pull off a successful hostage rescue mission at the airport in Entebbe, Uganda, in 1976. Failed diplomacy and poor use of military force left Carter running on empty. An American president was now helpless to influence events to reach a successful conclusion. Each action you take should lead to an outcome from which to implement your next action. It's like jumping from rock to rock across a stream—make sure you have enough rocks, or you are going to get wet. Carter got wet.

11. **Friends and Enemies**: When managing a crisis, the friends you have made and the goodwill you have created are assets, but issues management can be a very lonely endeavor when friends sit on the sidelines and enemies look for opportunities to use the crisis to their

advantage. Carter provided his adversaries with more ammunition to use against him. There are two outcomes to failure: Forgiveness and Blame. The skilled issues manager will position the issue where failure brings a second chance in the "lose-win" scenario while the unsuccessful issues manager will suffer a "lose-lose" outcome. Carter received no forgiveness when he failed.

In a speech at a fundraising event in Philadelphia in 1979, as reported in *The Washington Post*, Senator Ted Kennedy summed up the Carter presidency in a few sentences: "We want action, not excuses. We want leadership that inspires the people, not leadership that . . . blames the people for malaise." Carter was a competent man who lacked the ability to inspire people and build support. He was an engineer who saw problem-solving through the lens of process. He was a deeply religious man who viewed the world through the prism of morality and justice. These are admirable qualities that did not serve him well as an issues manager.

Carter would go on to have a successful post-presidency as a teacher and author. He created the Carter Center, which focuses on conflict resolution, health, human rights, and peace on a global scale. He also was a major factor in the expansion of Habitat for Humanity that builds affordable housing for the poor. Carter had a gift for organizing things to make them work better and a moral foundation that focused him on helping others. These gifts were better applied outside the presidency. He has certainly been one of the most consequential former presidents in our history.

Next up is Ronald Wilson Reagan and his conservative revolution.

CHAPTER 10

Reagan—Goodwill to the Rescue

Franz Kafka wrote: "It is impossible to defend oneself in the absence of goodwill." The power of goodwill is sometimes overlooked or undervalued when managing an issue. It is the "get of jail free" card that allows you to move on from mistakes and maintain a high level of support. Ronald Reagan would leverage the goodwill he had built during his presidency to manage a potentially disastrous crisis.

Ronald Wilson Reagan was born in Tampico, Illinois. He was athletic and handsome and very likeable. He became a Hollywood actor. Early in his career, he was involved with the Screen Actors Guild. He would serve as the organization's president during the McCarthy Era when several big-name stars, producers, directors, and screenwriters were called to testify in Washington about their involvement in or sympathies for the Communist Party.

These events, plus his disillusionment with Roosevelt's "New Deal" policies, moved Reagan to become a conservative and its most articulate spokesman. He would use his fame to campaign for Republican candidates in California and build his political base of support. In 1966, Reagan was elected governor of California and would serve two terms from 1967 to 1975.

Reagan's goal was to be president. He would enter the primaries late in 1968 against Richard Nixon. He won California, but party leaders decided he did not have sufficient broad-based support and nominated Nixon. In 1976, he challenged sitting president Gerald Ford for the nomination. Reagan by that time had established his political gravitas having been a two-term governor of California and he had a winning message of transformative conservative change. He did not win but ended his 1976 challenge as a force to be reckoned with in 1980.

The nomination would not be handed to Reagan in 1980. He faced a challenge from George H.W. Bush of Texas, but Reagan steamrolled to victory winning 44 states and nearly 60 percent of the Republican primary vote. The Republican Party had nominated its second conservative in 16 years. In the general election, Reagan would face a beleaguered president, Jimmy Carter. Reagan would carry 44 states and win 489 electoral votes in one of the most lopsided victories in American history against an incumbent president.

On January 20, 1981, Iran freed the 52 remaining American hostages who had been held for 444 days. This happened just minutes after President Reagan was sworn into office and delivered his address to the nation. The crisis that had paralyzed the Carter administration was finally over, but in its aftermath, a new challenge arose—terrorism.

In his first inaugural address, which is usually the clearest source in helping to understand how a new president intends to govern, Ronald Reagan:

1. **Stated the challenge**: "We suffer from the longest and one of the worst sustained inflations in our national history ... Idle industries have cast workers into unemployment, human misery, and personal indignity. Those who do work are denied a fair return for their labor by a tax system which penalizes successful achievement and keeps us from maintaining full productivity."

2. **Defined the goal**: "The economic ills we suffer have come upon us over several decades. They will not go away in days, weeks, or months, but they will go away. They will go away because we as Americans have the capacity now, as we've had in the past, to do whatever needs to be done to preserve this last and greatest bastion of freedom."

3. **Framed the problem**: "In this present crisis, government is not the solution to our problem; government is the problem. From time to time, we've been tempted to believe that society has become too complex to be managed by self-rule, that government by an elite group is superior to government for, by, and of the people."

4. **Projected optimism**: "We have every right to dream heroic dreams. Those who say that we're in a time when there are not heroes, they just don't know where to look. You can see heroes every day going

in and out of factory gates. Others, a handful in number, produce enough food to feed all of us and then the world beyond. You meet heroes across a counter, and they're on both sides of that counter. There are entrepreneurs with faith in themselves and faith in an idea who create new jobs, new wealth and opportunity."

These are two great lessons in issues management: Never define a challenge without stating a goal, and always frame a problem in optimistic terms. Reagan came to power with a strong mandate to act but not with a Republican Congress to help enact his vision into law.

Reagan's economic plan was called Reaganomics and included "widespread tax cuts, decreased social spending, increased military spending, and the deregulation of domestic markets." He faced strong headwinds as inflation would not surrender easily, and the United States was in recession creating high unemployment.

Going into the 1982 midterm elections, President Reagan's poll numbers had sunk from 57 percent in 1981 to 43 percent, according to Gallup. He would lead his party into the 1982 midterm elections with a promise to "stay the course."

The New York Times reported on the consequences of the 1982 election, writing: "The Democrats expanded their majority in the House of Representatives by 26 votes Tuesday in an election that raised doubts about President Reagan's ability to protect his conservative economic program from alteration by Congress." The report also cited that the balance in the House had been upended because the election "removed about 24 conservatives from the delicately balanced bipartisan coalition that helped pass Mr. Reagan's key economic legislation." Tip O'Neill called it "A Disastrous Defeat."

In issues management, sticking to your mandate is sometimes the right call. The nation was not used to conservative governance, and Reagan had not yet produced the results he had promised. The midterm elections for Reagan would prove to be a "lose-win" outcome from which he could continue his fight.

Likability and positivity were two of Reagan's greatest assets. He drew people into his orbit and was not viewed as an enemy, but rather as someone who viewed the world through a different lens. He disagreed but was not disagreeable. He was tough but fair. He was honest and forthright. These are the personal qualities that positioned Reagan for success as an issues manager.

Reagan would have a productive two years after the midterms. Congress passed a gas tax increase, strategic defense initiative, social security reforms, and his final tax cut. Also, the recession came to an end. In October 1983, Reagan would fight a splendid little war against Grenada. In his State of the Union address in 1983, he pushed Congress to cut the deficit. Reagan's brand of conservatism was still alive and kicking.

In 1984, Reagan would face Walter Mondale who was a former senator from Minnesota and had also served as Jimmy Carter's vice president. Reagan believed in supply-side economics. This is a theory that claims tax cuts for the wealthy result in increased savings and investment that trickles down to help the overall economy. Reagan's critics called his approach "voodoo" economics. In order to differentiate himself from Reagan, Mondale released his economic plan. *The New York Times* quoted Mondale as saying: "Mr. Reagan, all my cards are on the table, face up," and went on say, "Americans are calling your hand. Let's see it. Let's debate it." The reporting went on to point out: "The Mondale plan calls for $85 billion in new taxes which would fall heaviest on the wealthiest Americans."

Reagan would carry all but one state on his way to winning 525 electoral votes. The Reagan landslide would not carry the House of Representatives that Democrats would organize with a 254 to 181 majority, but Republicans remained in control of the Senate 53 to 47. With his strong reelection mandate, Reagan's approval rose to 60 percent in his second term.

In his second inaugural address, he would:

1. **Take a Bow**: "By 1980, we knew it was time to renew our faith ... We believed then and now there are no limits to growth and human progress when men and women are free to follow their dreams. And we were right to believe that. Tax rates have been reduced, inflation cut dramatically, and more people are employed than ever before in our history. We are creating a nation once again vibrant, robust, and alive."

2. **Define America's Global Mission**: "We strive for peace and security, heartened by the changes all around us ... Human freedom is on the march ... People, worldwide, hunger for the right of self-determination, for those inalienable rights that make for human dignity and progress. America must remain freedom's staunchest friend, for freedom is our best ally."

Reagan was a staunch anti-communist. He would start an arms race with the passage of the Strategic Defense Initiative, known as "Star Wars," that he knew Russia could not match. He boldly and openly spoke of freedom abroad and he set in motion a series of events that would lead to the fall of the Berlin Wall in 1989 and the collapse of the Soviet Union in 1991. Reagan was "sneaky strong" in foreign policy. He often used humor and a good-natured approach to life to mask the fact that he was a tough negotiator, and everyone knew exactly where he stood.

Clarity is one of your greatest assets in issues management to bring your supporters along with you. Reagan often linked many of his policies to greater, societal values that were easier to support by the American people. His brand of conservatism also appropriated American imagery like the flag. He branded his image to that of America. The lesson here is linking to widely accepted values and images can propel your issues management to the next level.

On May 1, 1985, Reagan instituted a trade embargo on the Central American nation of Nicaragua. This is a nation of approximately six million people whose major export is coffee and whose population is mainly uneducated with vast income disparities. Like in Cuba before Castro, the United States had great influence in Nicaragua.

The Sandinistas were a "Nicaraguan political party founded in the early 1960s with two primary goals: rooting out U.S. imperialism and establishing a socialist society modeled after the Cuban Revolution." Like Castro in Cuba and the Viet Cong in Vietnam, they were an insurgency group within a nation that promoted nationalism. In 1979, they came to power after the Battle for Managua and took control of the government. Daniel Ortega was the new leader of Nicaragua. An opposition counterinsurgency then formed that was called Contra or counter-revolutionaries. Once again, the threat of communism expanding into the Western Hemisphere was real, and the "domino effect" was still operational as an organizing principle. This was happening on Reagan's watch. He, like John F. Kennedy before him, would seek to topple a communist regime.

Peter Kornbluh wrote of the Reagan administration's covert war: "The strategy was to force the Sandinistas to become in reality what [U.S.] administration officials called them rhetorically: aggressive abroad, repressive at home, and hostile to the United States." Predictably, when the CIA-backed Contras began to engage in sabotage in 1982— blowing up a bridge near the Honduran border—the Sandinistas reacted with repressive measures, which confirmed the Reagan administration's branding of them.

Ortega arguably was no Fidel Castro: "The Sandinistas fashioned themselves as a democratic movement. Instead of defining democracy in terms of elections, the FSLN, (Sandinista National Liberation Front) believed that democracy meant popular support and participation."

The fall of Iran to theocrats and the rise of the Sandinistas in Nicaragua happened in the same year. Terrorism was the new threat that grew out of the first event and the spread of communism was the implied threat that was presented in the second. Reagan was willing to risk political capital to rid Central America of communism.

In June 1982:

> The birth of the Reagan Doctrine is publicly announced. This is Reagan's foreign policy that established support for democratiza- tion in countries engaged in socialist revolutions. Thus, the goal of covert operations in Nicaragua shifts from one of ostensibly interdicting arms, to one of supporting a change in government.

The CIA would become actively involved in an effort to overthrow the government of Nicaragua.

Congress responded by enacting the Boland Amendment. It pro- hibited the federal government from providing military support "for the purpose of overthrowing the Government of Nicaragua." It aimed at preventing CIA funding of rebels opposed to the revolutionary pro- visional junta in Nicaragua. Basically, the Contras were now on their own according to Congress. The Boland Amendments, there would be two, were basically a showdown between the president's power to conduct foreign policy and the power of Congress to fund it. Reagan is quoted as saying in response that he will: "keep the Contras together body and soul, no matter what Congress voted for."

On September 22, 1980, the Iran and Iraq war started. It would last 10 years. There was a U.S. embargo on selling weapons to Iran as fallout from the hostage crisis. Iran was able to buy weapons from other countries. Compounding matters was that seven U.S. citizens were being held hostage by Hezbollah, an Iranian-backed militia group, in Lebanon. Perfect storm. The political calculus was to find a way to sell weapons and spare parts to Iran to build goodwill and then leverage this goodwill to secure the release of the hostages by its proxy. The plan would involve Israel as the intermediary to facilitate the sale. The plan on the surface seemed to be a "win-win."

There is an issues management problem called making "soup by committee." This is when everyone gets to add ingredients as they see fit. This is how a "win-win" can quickly be transformed into a "lose-lose." In the end you have really bad soup and no one is responsible for making it because everyone made it.

The Reagan administration still had a Contra funding problem. It was actively raising private money to fund the rebels, but now a plan would be hatched to get more money and weapons to the rebels. The plan, as special counsel Lawrence Walsh would write, was to "conduct foreign policy off the books." Reagan's administration was undertaking a proxy war in Central America using the Contras against the Cuban-backed Sandinistas. The problem was he had no way to support his proxy army.

Within the framework of arms sales to Iran, Lt. Col. Oliver North hatched a plan where he would put an additional mark-up on the weapons and use it to buy and ship weapons to the Contra rebels. North, it would be reported, was conducting his own foreign policy saying things like "Saddam Hussein must go." Foreign policy is very complex because the interests of nations are multifaceted. It could be argued that this is why the plan began to unravel.

The more complex the issue, the more interests are in play. These interests are often in conflict, or there is a value mismatch where one party values something more highly than the other. This creates a lot of trip wires. Trust is very difficult to maintain in this environment. It also makes it easier for third-party deals to be cut. Remember Gabriel Man-igault's political credo, "the enemy of my enemy is my friend," and you will be well served.

On November 3, 1986, the "arms for hostages" plan was initially reported in Ash-Shiaa, a Lebanese magazine. Its reporting was based on a leak from a high-ranking member of Iran's revolutionary guard. Shortly thereafter a plane, loaded with arms intended for the Contra, crashed in Nicaragua. The pilot, who survived the crash, admitted to working for the Central Intelligence Agency (CIA). On November 13, 1986, President Reagan addressed the nation from the Oval Office. He framed the issue this way:

> For 18 months now we have had underway a secret diplomatic initiative to Iran. That initiative was undertaken for the simplest and best of reasons: to renew a relationship with the nation of Iran, to bring an honorable end to the bloody 6-year war between Iran and Iraq, to eliminate state-sponsored terrorism and subversion, and to affect the safe return of all hostages.

In his address he did not mention how the arms deal was helping the Contras.

On November 25, 1986, the controversy reached a higher level when "Attorney General Meese announced that the arms sales proceeds were diverted to fund Nicaraguan rebels—the Contras—who were fighting a guerrilla war against the elected leftist government of Nicaragua."

Reagan denied knowledge of money flowing to the Contras, but he then fired Lt. Col. North and Admiral Poindexter who was then his national security adviser under whom North worked. On December 19, 1986, Lawrence Walsh was appointed by the court as special counsel in charge of the Iran-Contra investigation. He would spend the next six years trying to connect the dots of exactly what happened and who was responsible for breaking the law and conducting foreign policy off book.

On December 1, 1986, the Tower Commission was approved by Reagan to look into the matter. It would report in 1987 that "Reagan's disengagement from the management of his White House had created conditions which made possible the diversion of funds to the Contras.

But there was no evidence linking Reagan to the diversion." *The New York Times* would report:

> In unusually blunt language, the board placed direct blame on Donald T. Regan, the White House chief of staff, and other advisers for giving the President poor advice and neglecting to grasp "the serious legal and political risks" of the arms deal and the subsequent diversion of profits to the Nicaraguan rebels, known as Contras.

On March 4, 1987, President Reagan addressed the nation on Iran-Contra in the wake of the Tower Commission Report:

1. **Took Responsibility**: "First, let me say I take full responsibility for my own actions and for those of my administration. As angry as I may be about activities undertaken without my knowledge, I am still accountable for those activities. As disappointed as I may be in some who served me, I'm still the one who must answer to the American people for this behavior. And as personally distasteful as I find secret bank accounts and diverted funds—well, as the Navy would say, this happened on my watch."

2. **Reframed Arms Deal**: "A few months ago I told the American people I did not trade arms for hostages. My heart and my best intentions still tell me that's true, but the facts and the evidence tell me it is not … It's clear from the Board's report, however, that I let my personal concern for the hostages spill over into the geopolitical strategy of reaching out to Iran."

3. **Plan of Action**: "I endorse every one of the Tower board's recommendations. In fact, I'm going beyond its recommendations so as to put the house in even better order. I'm taking action in three basic areas: personnel, national security policy, and the process for making sure that the system works." Reagan would bring a new team into the White House, order an investigation of all covert operations, and change how the National Security Council worked.

4. **Move Forward**: "Now, what should happen when you make a mistake is this: You take your knocks, you learn your lessons, and then

you move on. That's the healthiest way to deal with a problem. This in no way diminishes the importance of the other continuing investigations, but the business of our country and our people must proceed."

Reagan's political instincts served him well in this crisis. He knew there was a benefit in acting first when an investigation is inevitable. He let the facts come out without applying pressure or interfering with investigations. He did not view those investigating him as his adversaries. He did not question their motives. He let the process play out. As a leader, there are issues that you will need to allow to play out in their own time without any help from you.

The work of special counsel Lawrence Walsh's investigation would continue unimpeded for six years. The results included:

14 persons were charged with criminal offenses. Eleven persons were convicted, but two convictions were overturned on appeal. Two persons were pardoned before trial and one case was dismissed when the (George H.W.) Bush Administration declined to declassify information necessary for trial. On December 24, 1992, President George H.W. Bush pardoned Caspar W. Weinberger, Duane R. Clarridge, Clair E. George, Elliott Abrams, Alan D. Fiers, Jr., and Robert C. McFarlane.

In the aftermath of the scandal, in 1987, Congress banned all but nonlethal support for the Contras. Without arms the war ended in a cease-fire in 1990. The scandal was over.

The lesson here is that bad news can be successfully managed. Reagan managed, unlike Richard Nixon, a complex issue that could have sunk his presidency had it been handled differently. He would take an initial hit in popularity, but it did not last long. He would leave office in January 1989 as the second most popular president, behind only Franklin D. Roosevelt.

Lessons

At Issue: Under the Reagan administration, laws were broken when an illegal arms deal with Iran resulted in funds being siphoned off to fund a counter-revolutionary group in Nicaragua whose goal was to overthrow a communist-leaning government.

Lesson: President Reagan's crisis teaches the value of getting out in front when bad news is coming and adjusting as new facts are introduced.

1. **Brushfires**: In issues management it is always wise to extinguish fires early. Evidence began to mount that Iran-Contra was becoming an issue. Reagan did not hope that it would go away or create a denial narrative. Instead, he opted into a transparent process to find the facts by appointing the Tower Commission. This is an example of best practice.

2. **Means Justify the End**: In issues management, having a worthy goal does not give you permission to reach it using any means available. Some in Reagan's administration were all-in supporting the Contra even though to support them meant breaking the law. Stay within defined boundaries because a flawed process can quickly derail a good strategy. It may take more time, but doing things the right way is best.

3. **Too Many Cooks**: Iran-Contra had a lot of chefs in the kitchen, each claiming to be working under the authority of the president. In issues management, this starts to create the problem of "authority creep," where decisions are made to advance a goal with no one really in charge. This is where authority and responsibility are misaligned. When the two disconnect, the cohesion of an organization quickly begins to fray, and finger-pointing will quickly follow. If someone has been designated by the leader to carry out a task, make sure that it is crystal clear to everyone that the person has specific authority and where that authority came from.

4. **Added Steps**: In all issues management, you want to assess whether the goal is worth the risks it takes to achieve it. In Iran-Contra there were a lot of moving pieces, and achieving the goal of a successful Contra counter-revolution was not under the administration's direct control. In issues management there are three circles. The first contains what you can control. The second are things you can influence. The third holds those things you can't control but would like to influence. In steps 2 and 3, actions do not assure that the results will be as expected. All tactics should be placed into one of these

three circles in order to provide a fair assessment of the extent of your influence to shape events and the likelihood of success resulting from your actions.

5. **Rube Goldberg**: In issues management try to avoid creating a "Tower of Babel" by constructing a Rube Goldberg strategy to manage an issue. The simpler and more understandable you can keep your strategy, the more success you will have in bringing it to a favorable conclusion. Examine each step of your strategy and make sure that you and your team can explain the rationale for taking it. If you reach a point where you cannot produce statements that express clear understandings, then reassess your strategy.

6. **Known-Unknowns**: The more people involved, the greater the chance something will be made public that can undermine strategy. There were so many moving parts in Iran-Contra, and too many people knew a lot about what was going on, but only a few had the whole story. The leak that would start the dominoes falling was a report in a Lebanese newspaper from a source in Iran's Republican Guard. Humans do not keep secrets very well. Keeping track of who knows what and who is a threat because they know too little is a good practice to follow. Regular meetings with key staff is a best practice in keeping everyone connected and informed.

7. **Fess Up**: At first Reagan said he knew nothing about Iran-Contra. Denying a foreign policy blunder of this magnitude meant that Reagan was either a really bad manager or he was not telling the truth. In issues management, accept the fact that you knew something carries less penalty than denying you knew anything. You can shape what you know, but a false denial brings into question your veracity.

8. **Shine a Light**: Reagan's response to Iran-Contra was to immediately create the Tower Commission to investigate it and cooperate with the special counsel by releasing the documents he requested. In issues management, transparency is always the preferable approach. Investigations and commissions buy you time. Sometimes a little more time is all you need. Reagan acted in the opposite manner to Nixon in Watergate and his initial transparency reinforced the public perception that he was acting in good faith and had nothing to hide.

9. **Have a Plan**: After the Tower Commission reported its findings, President Reagan went on television and owned up to being wrong initially. In issues management owning the problem is only one part of getting to a successful conclusion. The second piece is to create an action plan to make the solution operational. There are two phases in issues management: Moving to and moving on. When Reagan outlined his three reforms, he was not only taking responsibility but he was also providing assurances that something like this will not happen again on his watch.

10. **Eyes on the Road**: As the leader, you have the ultimate responsibility in managing an issue. Reagan arguably was a hands-off executive who had his focus on the release of the hostages and not on the details of how the entire operation was playing out. In issues management, organizational alignment is not optional. Issues develop quicky and trip up a team that is not aligned. When you need a detail guy then appoint one. If you need a big-picture thinker, then hire one. Know your team and the skills they bring to the project.

11. **Off With His Head**: There are good and bad times in which you make decisions in issues management. A good rule of thumb is that the higher the heat, the more necessary it is to buy time. When this issue first broke, it had the potential to steamroll the Reagan administration. If the issue had been allowed to move at its own pace, then Reagan may have faced much more lethal political options. The Tower Commission put the issue on the right track and positioned Reagan as a man of action trying to solve a problem. The action of appointing the commission was just as important as what the commission found. Reagan's initial action set the right tone and positioned him to control the politics of the issue going forward.

12. **Cooler Heads**: Never underestimate the value of having good people on your team. In issues management, the strong keep their focus and the weak panic. As the issue is being sorted out, you want to have people who can stay calm and accurately assess what is happening during the most difficult times.

13. **Leaving the Mess**: Most of the reports on the investigation into Iran-Contra would come late in Reagan's administration. The time he gained through good issues management allowed him to maintain

most of his popularity. It would be President George H.W. Bush who would be left to clean up the mess by issuing pardons to those involved. In issues management, there are times when one team is able to skirt the fallout and leave the mess for the next team to deal with. It is important to understand that issues management does not happen in a defined time framework. Often, timelines are extended, blame recalculated, and the mess left for others to clean up.

Ronald Reagan was never indicted for Iran-Contra, but it was a stain on his administration, albeit not a big enough stain to undo the image Reagan had created through his words and actions as an effective leader who brought American out of the malaise of the 1970s. People remember the big things, and Ronald Reagan provided enough big things that Iran-Contra became only a footnote in his presidency.

Next, we will look at one of the more qualified men ever to serve as president in terms of the variety of positions he held before he was elected president—George H.W. Bush.

CHAPTER 11

Bush 41—Goal Achieved

Russian author Alexander Solzhenitsyn provided a valuable lesson in issues management when he pointed out the limits of power: "You only have power over people as long as you don't take everything away from them." In issues management, those you select to bring under your tent will help you advance your issues on their terms not your terms. George H.W. Bush understood this lesson and applied it when removing Saddam Hussein's army that was occupying Kuwait.

Ronald Reagan is a beloved figure in the Republican Party. He was the first conservative in the modern era to govern the United States. He was also a consequential president. British prime minister Margaret Thatcher, his staunch ally, wrote that Reagan had "achieved the most difficult of all political tasks: changing attitudes and perceptions about what is possible." A true leader is someone who possesses the ability to understand those he leads and provide them with the foundation and encouragement to grow.

Reagan's vice president throughout his two terms was George H.W. Bush. He was born into a prominent New England family. He attended Phillips Academy Andover and Yale University where he was a star athlete and an exceptional student. On his 18th birthday in 1942, he enlisted in the U.S. Navy, became a pilot, and flew 58 combat missions. He was the youngest pilot in the Navy in World War II. On his last mission his airplane was shot down. He was rescued and received the Distinguished Flying Cross.

After the war and graduating Yale University, Bush moved to Texas, where he was in the oil business. He founded Zapata Petroleum, which is now part of HRG Group which is a $5.2 billion enterprise. He would be elected to Congress in 1966. He would mount an unsuccessful run for the U.S. Senate in 1970, after which he would be appointed ambassador to the United Nations by President Nixon. He would move over to head the Republican National Committee in 1973 and was appointed envoy to the People's Republic of China by President Gerald R. Ford, where he stayed for two years and then returned to Washington to lead the Central Intelligence Agency until 1977.

Bush ran for president in 1980 against Ronald Reagan. It was he who claimed that Reagan's economic proposals were "voodoo economics." Reagan swept the nomination. It was now time to choose a vice president. According to a piece written by Richard V. Allen that was published in *The New York Times Magazine*, there was a deal on the table to have Reagan pick former president Gerald Ford as his running mate. The deal came with a lot of strings that initially included the demand that Henry Kissinger be appointed Secretary of State as well as having several other Ford loyalists appointed to key positions. Reagan was uncomfortable with the deal. When asked about Bush, Reagan said: "I can't take him; that 'voodoo economic' policy charge and his stand on abortion are wrong." The demands of the Ford team were too much and negotiations with them began to break down. He called Bush and asked him if he would support the entire Republican platform. When Bush agreed, he became Reagan's pick. Bush was known for his integrity, loyalty, and knowledge of foreign policy. He would balance the ticket, because by many, he was a moderating influence on Reagan.

Bush ran for president in 1988. In the primary election, Bush would be challenged by Senator Bob Dole of Kansas. There were conservatives who believed, even after eight years as Reagan's vice president, that Bush was not a dependable conservative. Dole would win five primary contests and 20 percent of the vote. Bush promised a "kinder and gentler" nation and to continue Reagan's policies. He won the nomination. In the general election, Bush faced Michael Dukakis, whom he branded as the liberal governor of Massachusetts. It stuck. Bush would run the infamous "Willie Horton Ad" that accused Dukakis of being soft on crime. Bush carried 40 states and won 426 electoral votes.

In his inaugural address on January 20, 1989, he outlined:

1. **Reagan's Victory**: "We know what works: Freedom works. We know what's right: Freedom is right. We know how to secure a more just and prosperous life for man on Earth: through free markets, free speech, free elections, and the exercise of free will unhampered by the state."

2. **Stated Governing Principles**: "America is never wholly herself unless she is engaged in high moral principle. We as a people have such a purpose today. It is to make kinder the face of the Nation and gentler the face of the world. My friends, we have work to do. There are the homeless, lost and roaming."

3. **Starting Point**: "I have spoken of a thousand points of light, of all the community organizations that are spread like stars throughout the Nation, doing good. We will work hand in hand, encouraging, sometimes leading, sometimes being led, rewarding. We will work on this in the White House, in the Cabinet agencies. I will go to the people and the programs that are the brighter points of light, and I will ask every member of my government to become involved. The old ideas are new again because they are not old, they are timeless: duty, sacrifice, commitment, and a patriotism that finds its expression in taking part and pitching in."

The world was moving away from the old black-and-white paradigm where communism was the existential threat to freedom and democracy. Communism had stalled in its global expansion. The fears of the "domino effect" that had shaped the policies of several administrations had failed to materialize. Reagan's hard line on communism was about to pay huge dividends. In 1989, the Berlin Wall, a physical barrier that divided east from west Berlin for 28 years, came down, and a united Germany was reborn. And,

> On December 25, 1991, the Soviet flag flew over the Kremlin in Moscow for the last time. Representatives from Soviet republics (Ukraine, Georgia, Belarus, Armenia, Azerbaijan, Kazakhstan, Kyrgyzstan, Moldova, Turkmenistan, Tajikistan, and Uzbekistan) had already announced that they would no longer be part of the Soviet Union. Instead, they declared they would establish a Commonwealth of Independent States.

Bush would refer to these events as having created a "new world order" that created a different global geography and new global challenges than his predecessors faced. The Cold War, which had existed since the end of World War II, was now over.

In issues management, it is often true that the harvest from the seeds planted by a predecessor is enjoyed by those who follow. Some of the work done by Reagan was not realized by him during his presidency. This is why it is important to take a long view in issues management rather than only seek immediate results. Conversely, Reagan also left unfinished business for Bush, who had to bailout savings and loans that were overextended under Reagan and clean up the mess in the wake of Iran-Contra.

Bush's main challenges would be global. America was now the beacon of freedom for fledgling democracies and the world's only superpower. A nation like Poland wanted U.S. support and guidance to get its democracy on track. Also, in China, there were pro-democracy protests. In Tiananmen Square, the Chinese army violently suppressed the protests using tanks. It is estimated that 1,000 freedom protesters were killed. But as communism subsided, a new challenge emerged—global terrorism and the rise of a radical brand of Islam.

Saddam Hussein was the leader of Iraq. He was a member of the Ba'ath Party which was part nationalist and part socialist. He assumed power in 1976 and used strongman and authoritarian rule to keep the nation from devolving into warring factions. Hussein would go to war with Iran in 1980 "to remove Khomeini from power and replace his regime with one more friendly to Iraq." One key development in this war was Iraq's use of chemical weapons. As documented by Jevid Ali, "By early 1988, Iraq began conducting offensives to recapture territory using CW (chemical weapons)."

The war ended with a cease-fire overseen by the United Nations in 1990. But Saddam won in a way by positioning himself as the predominant Arab leader:

> As nearly all Arab nations had supported Iraq during the war in order to contain Iran, Iraq emerged from the conflict with more power in the region than it had before, fueled by a strengthened military and the ruthless ambition of its leader.

This emboldened Hussein who on August 2, 1990, ordered the invasion of Kuwait.

In a series of propaganda moves, Saddam accused Kuwait of doing an end run on The Organization of the Petroleum Exporting States (OPEC)

deal that limited oil sales, stealing oil from Iraqi oil fields using slant drilling, and of being an ancient province of Iraq. "In reality, Saddam owed
the Kuwaitis $14 billion from Iraq's nearly 10-year war with Iran and
Kuwaiti oil drilling was driving down the price of oil." It took only two
days for Iraq to conquer Kuwait. The occupation force was estimated at
between 400,000 and 500,000 troops, and there was fear that he would
move on from Kuwait to invade Saudi Arabia. This action would have
completely disrupted the global economy.

On August 7, 1990, President George Herbert Walker Bush ordered
the organization of Operation Desert Shield in response to Iraq's invasion
of Kuwait less than a week earlier. He would build the "coalition of the
willing" consisting of 48 nations, including several Arab nations and stage
500,000 troops in the Middle East to drive Hussein's army out of Kuwait.

On September 11, 1990, President Bush spoke before a joint session
of Congress stating, as reported in *Politico*: "Iraq will not be permitted
to annex Kuwait," Bush told the lawmakers in the presence of foreign
diplomats, including the Iraqi ambassador. "And that's not a threat, not a
boast. It's just the way it's going to be."

"Out of these troubled times," Bush went on to say, "... a new world
order can emerge: a new era, freer from the threat of terror, stronger in the
pursuit of justice and more secure in the quest for peace."

President Bush was smart not to position this statement as only a
threat. Like Kennedy's statement after the Bay of Pigs, Bush framed that
action in a larger context of creating a "new world order" that would be
based in cooperation among nations to seek peace and end the threat of
terrorism.

"On November 29, 1990, the United Nations Security Council
authorized the use of 'all means necessary' to remove Hussein's forces
from Kuwait, giving Iraq the deadline of midnight on January 16, 1991,
to leave or risk forcible removal." On January 17, 1991, Operation Desert
Shield became Operation Desert Storm. Its sole focus was the use of force
to remove Saddam Hussein from Kuwait

Bombing would last for about six weeks. The invasion would last only
four days. It was traditional warfare where two armies met on the field of
battle. It was also a rout. Coalition forces would lose a total of 147 com-
batants, either killed in battle or dying of battle wounds. In all, there were
about 1,100 coalition casualties. Estimates of Iraqi casualties approached

150,000. General Colin Powell put it bluntly: "Our strategy in going after this army is very simple. First, we are going to cut it off, and then we are going to kill it." The operation would deploy an overwhelming force to achieve its strategic objective of driving the Iraqi army out of Kuwait. It worked.

On February 27, 1991, President Bush addressed the nation because Hussein, although his army was defeated, refused to concede. Bush warned:

> The coalition will therefore continue to prosecute the war with undiminished intensity. As we announced last night, we will not attack unarmed soldiers in retreat. We have no choice but to consider retreating combat units as a threat and respond accordingly.

He went on to ask Iraqi soldiers to lay down their arms. They did in vast numbers and surrendered.

On February 28, 1991, *The New York Times* reported: "Declaring that 'Kuwait is liberated' and Iraq's army defeated, President Bush ordered allied forces on Wednesday night to suspend offensive military operations against President Saddam Hussein's isolated and battered army." Subsequently,

> April 3 the U.N. Security Council passed Resolution 687, specifying conditions for a formal end to the conflict. According to the resolution, Bush's cease-fire would become official, some sanctions would be lifted, but the ban on Iraqi oil sales would continue until Iraq destroyed its weapons of mass destruction under U.N. supervision. On April 6, Iraq accepted the resolution, and on April 11 the Security Council declared it in effect.

The fight was over for now.

In issues management, conditions are often attached to resolution. These are commitments made by one or both sides in a dispute that lists what each party is required to do. Conditions can often create the foundation for new issues to arise in the future, but they settle the issue that is in dispute presently. A conditional solution may be the best you are able to achieve, but it is important that all items are clearly stated, and a process is put in place to confirm that all conditions have been fulfilled.

President Bush would enjoy an approval rating of 89 percent on February 28, 1991. It would fall to 29 percent on July 16, 1992, as candidate Bill Clinton's team pounded Bush on the economy. It would stay low through Election Day, and according to Gallup:

> In slightly more than a year's time, Bush had gone from having the highest job approval rating to one of the lowest Gallup has measured, only slightly better than the readings in the mid-to-low 20s Harry Truman and Richard Nixon received at the end of their presidencies.

The Persian Gulf War caused oil prices to spike. This accelerated inflation caused by the rapid growth in government spending under Reagan and the tighter money policies instituted in response to the savings and loan defaults resulting in an economic contraction. Under President Reagan, federal outlays had gone for $746 billion to $1.144 trillion in eight years.

George H.W. Bush organized and led a great coalition to victory against Iraq. It was the first shot in a new war that would consume America for the next 30 years.

Lessons

At Issue: President George H.W. Bush achieved his military objective to remove Iraqi military forces from Kuwait and ended the war.

Lesson: President George H.W. Bush teaches us the value of setting goals and defining victory to avoid mission creep when managing an issue.

1. **Seeing the Field**: President Bush understood the vast global consequences of a Middle East controlled by Saddam Hussein and chose Kuwait to stop this from happening. In issues management, there are problems that will clearly grow much larger, and their negative impacts will become more serious if not addressed immediately. Issues need to be prioritized not only based on the immediate

impacts, but also on their ability to morph into greater problems or perpetuate a crisis down the road. The choice to act is often difficult, but the costs of delay can be much higher.

2. **State Clear Goals**: The goal of this war was not to remove Saddam from power or to conquer Iraq. The goal was to remove Iraqi occupation forces from Kuwait. This limited the scope and made it easier for other nations to support the effort. In issues management, you need to remain true to the deal you cut with other parties, even when new opportunities present themselves. Bush could have destroyed the Iraqi army as it retreated, but this would have created other issues going forward. Coalition partners agreed to support United States in reaching a specific goal that aligned with their self-interests. To go beyond that agreement would have put allies at risk.

3. **Build External Support**: When managing issues, an "us versus them" fight can open the door for unanticipated problems as new alliances form. The more you can expand your support, the more credibility you build around your approach to finding a solution. President Bush went to the United Nations for both approval and permission to move forward with his plan to oust Saddam. Getting its approval gave him moral high ground and opened the door for others to join the cause. Had Bush tried to undertake this mission alone, it would have closed more doors than it opened and left him isolated.

4. **Transfer Authority**: The other side of the same coin of using an external authority is you have relinquished some authority but assume all risk. Working under the auspices of the United Nations meant that the conditions of victory would not be determined by or enforced by the United States. Had something like the United Nations conducted World War II, then it would not have been President Truman's decision to use the atomic bomb on Japan and end the war. When managing issues, be aware that when you use the authority of others, you lose a measure of autonomy.

5. **Build Assets**: Third-party approval can broaden your appeal. In most conflicts, there are the good guys and the bad guys and the side of right and the side of wrong. The work Bush did in advance of military action was brilliant and necessary. In issues management,

constructing the plan of action and building support in advance can be an invaluable asset.

6. **Assure Success**: Using overwhelming force was another key to success. The United States did not present half-measures to its allies. Every non-nuclear weapon in our arsenal was on the table, as was our open checkbook. This lowered the risk for the allies as they were able to sell to their stakeholders that whatever military action was taken, it would be short and decisive. In issues management the alpha-leader leads and makes it easy for others to follow.

7. **Declare Victory**: Victory has many faces. It is always good practice to state clearly what victory or success looks like at the beginning. Open-ended understandings can result in wasted time and resources and lead to mission creep. Changing the goal posts will often result in frustration internally and lost support from allies. It would have been easy for Bush to destroy Saddam's army as it retreated, but this was not the mission, and this use of force would have isolated Bush for other leaders. This was counter to his stated objective of creating a "new world order." Cooperation was the essential first step in managing these extremely sensitive and potentially dangerous issues.

8. **Leaving Embers**: Although Bush did stop the war from becoming a slaughter of Iraqi troops, he did leave behind embers that would create new fires in the future. Saddam had been humiliated but was still in power. Eisenhower did not solve civil rights issues, but he did draw a clear line that defined the federal response when civil rights were denied to minority students. Bush demonstrated that there is global resolve to confront terror and establish order in the Middle East. The challenge going forward would be how to maintain this commitment in the face of an evolving threat.

9. **Creating New Issues**: According to the French think tank Foundation for L'Innovation Politique, "between 1979 and 2019, at least 33,769 Islamist terrorist attacks took place worldwide. They caused the deaths of at least 167,096 people." The war had achieved its stated objective, but it did not solve all the problems in the Middle East. The message it sent to rulers like Saddam was that you can't win a big war. The response from Islamists was we will instead fight small battles at a time and place of our choosing. Postaction analysis

in issues management is especially important to game out the cost of victory or the price of failure. There will be fallout from any actions taken. It is best to assess it, define it, and be ready to act when it happens.

10. **Score to Settle**: Our forces were part of a larger coalition, but it was our military that was driving Iraq out of Kuwait. In defeat there is often more unity among the vanquished. A losing sports team will come closer together when they share a loss. Our military involvement in the Middle East in liberating Kuwait was just beginning. In issues management, the "win-lose" is potentially the most unwanted result. In it, you get what you want in the near term and sow the seeds for other conflicts down the road. Leaving scores to settle as an outcome is not best practice.

11. **All Fame Is Fleeting**: Politically, Bush was on top after the victory over Iraqi forces. His approval was 89 percent. But the flow of issues does not stop because you are busy fighting a war. A recession hit the U.S. economy, and although Americans felt good about what our forces had achieved, they soon turned inward, and the focus shifted. In issues management, never take your eye off what is happening in other parts of your organization. The crisis may seem to be all-consuming but continue to assess other issues that are developing.

George H.W. Bush would pay a political price for not appearing to manage the recession in the United States. He would be branded as an out-of-touch patrician by Bill Clinton and lose the election in 1992. Americans were ready to turn the page on foreign conflicts and focus on matters at home.

Next up is Bill Clinton who was a successful president because he always got the politics right and had the ability to change course when needed.

CHAPTER 12

Clinton—Bouncing Back

Agility is a key asset in issues management. Microsoft founder Bill Gates captured the concept by stating: "Success today requires the agility and drive to constantly rethink, reinvigorate, react, and reinvent." One constant in issues management is that things will change suddenly, unexpectedly, and not always to your advantage. Having the ability as the leader to adapt to change and the flexibility operationally to manage it are invaluable assets. Bill Clinton would demonstrate superior agility after a smashing defeat in the 1994 midterm elections to save his presidency and win a second term in office.

By 1992, the Gulf War was in the rearview mirror, and Americans were focused on what was happening at home. Although the recession had ended the year prior, the American spirit of optimism had not fully recovered.

President Bush was challenged in the primary by Patrick J. Buchannan, who was a religious conservative, broadcaster, author, and pundit who had served in the Nixon, Ford, and Reagan administrations. Bush had broken his promise not to raise taxes. Conservatives never really trusted Bush, and now they would try to teach him a lesson.

Democrats were also facing identity issues, deciding whether to go hard left or run a more moderate candidate. In their field were Bill Clinton, governor of Arkansas; Jerry Brown, liberal governor of California; and Senator Paul Tsongas of Massachusetts. Clinton had led the Democratic Leadership Council. It was a centrist organization focused on moving the Democratic Party to the middle politically.

Clinton's big break politically happened when he was chosen to speak at the Democratic National Convention in 1988, where he gave a long-winded, unfocused speech that *The Washington Post* panned as dreadful. Chris Wallace, then at NBC news, said Clinton "has gone on so long that he has completely lost this crowd.... It seems Bill Clinton has overstayed his welcome." Rather than be chased out of public life by one bad performance, Clinton embraced it, cultivating an image as likeable, smart, and a different kind of Democrat than most Americans were used to at that time.

There was also a third-party candidate, H. Ross Perot, who was a computer services billionaire. His focus was on the national debt. In 1933, where this book starts, the national debt was $23 billion. At the end of World War II, it stood at $239 billion. When Johnson began to expand U.S. commitment to the war in Vietnam in 1965, it totaled $317 billion. When President Reagan cut taxes in 1981, the debt stood at $998 billion, and after his last budget in 1989, it had grown to a staggering $2.6 trillion. In 1992, the deficit was an astounding $4.065 trillion.

Clinton would carry 32 states to Bush's 18 on his way to winning 370 electoral votes. Perot would carry no state, but he did win 19,743,821 votes and was a factor in the election. Many at first believed Perot lost the election for Bush. Post-election polling disputed this claim, but there is no doubt that it would have been a very different contest had it only been Clinton versus Bush. One key fact about the general election is that Bill Clinton won only 43 percent of the vote, so he did not have a clear mandate to govern.

Hillary Rodham was a graduate of Wellesley College and Yale Law School. She and Bill met at Yale. The Clintons shared a love of politics. They were both "children of the 1960s" who were very aware of the counter-culture movement. Hillary had a professional career before she was first lady as did Betty Ford who was a dancer and model, and Nancy Reagan who was an actress, but most first ladies did not have careers at the level of Hillary Rodham Clinton. During the campaign when Bill Clinton was questioned about how their relationship would work in the White House he replied, "You get two for the price of one." This implied that Hillary would be a partner in governing and not serve as a traditional first lady.

In his first inaugural address, Bill Clinton spelled out his mission:

To renew America, we must be bold. We must do what no generation has had to do before. We must invest more in our own people, in their jobs, in their future, and at the same time cut our massive debt. And we must do so in a world in which we must compete for every opportunity. It will not be easy; it will require sacrifice. But it can be done, and done fairly, not choosing to sacrifice for its own sake, but for our own sake. We must provide for our nation the way a family provides for its children.

How boldly would Bill Clinton govern the United States? He would show his hand soon—very soon after taking office.

On January 25, 1993, in his first major initiative as president, Bill Clinton announced that First Lady Hillary Clinton would lead a task-force to reform health care in America. *The New York Times* noted that this was the most powerful position to which a first lady had ever been appointed. The National Legal and Policy Center wrote:

There she was, the First Lady of the United States with the media and the entire Congressional leadership eating out of her hand. Flanked by Senators George Mitchell and Ted Kennedy in the Senate's Lyndon B. Johnson Conference Room, Hillary stood there as the only First Lady in history to confer with Congress on a crucial domestic policy issue.

This was a massive undertaking, so it would not be simple. There were also powerful interests involved, including health insurance companies and health care providers, and then there was the politics of the issue. Bill Clinton was immediately attacked on whether it was legal to appoint the first lady to lead a task force. On March 27 1993, *The New York Times* reported on the makeup of the secret task force writing: "Of the 511 people listed by the White House, 412 are described as full-time employees of the Government. 82 are described as special, or temporary, employees. And 17 are described as consultants." The newspaper went on to write: "More than 130 of those described as full-time Government employees work for members of Congress or for Congressional committees." The secrecy that surrounded the task force created a rumor mill. Eventually, the White House had to state publicly that the secret meetings "had nothing to do with some grand Soviet-style conspiracy."

The task force was vast, and it was bureaucratic. The National Legal and Policy Center wrote:

> The health plan itself was supposed to be unveiled May 30, 1993, to meet the President's much-ballyhooed 100-day deadline, but it was not officially presented to Congress until September 22, 1993. The task force was massively bureaucratic organized into fifteen so-called "Cluster Groups," forty-three "Working Groups" and four "Subgroups," task force participants had to pass their work through seven "tollgates" or check points.

What was in the 1,342-page plan? Paul Starr, writing a retrospective in *The American Prospect* about the "Hillary Care Plan," stated: "there seemed to be a historic opportunity to complete what Democrats had long regarded as the chief unfinished business of the "New Deal"—national health insurance." Bill Clinton talked about a national health care plan during the campaign in September 1992:

> The basic idea was not complicated. Consumers, not employers, would choose health plans. Firms would pay into a regional health insurance purchasing cooperative (later called an "alliance" in the Clinton plan), which would offer private plans of varying types to all residents under age 65 in an area (Medicare would remain separate). The alliances would be required to offer traditional, fee-for-service insurance as well as health maintenance organizations and preferred provider plans.

Starr went on to write:

> Benefits, copays, and other features would be standardized so as to make it easier for consumers to compare prices and get the best value for money. Health plans would have to offer coverage to everyone without exclusions of preexisting conditions, and they would be paid according to the characteristics of the population they enrolled.

When the plan was finished, Bill Clinton enjoined the nation, as reported by NBC News, "Our families will never be secure, our businesses will never be strong, and our government will never again be fully solvent until we tackle the health-care crisis. We must do it this year." The initiative would fail.

The Health Security Act, as it was officially known, was the biggest spending bill in half a century to come before Congress. It was met with broad based and diverse opposition from insurance companies, think tanks, and even within the Democratic Party. Senator Daniel Patrick Moynihan (D-NY) stated that "there is not a health care crisis there is an insurance crisis." There were also lawsuits, grassroots campaigns, and television ads designed to move public opinion to not support the proposed legislation. There were also budget concerns and competing legislative priorities to contend with in passing the bill.

Ballotpedia would list these reasons for the bill's failure politically: It was very large and difficult to explain; Clinton made little effort to win bipartisan support for the bill, and there were other pressing matters that demanded President Clinton's attention. Three such matters were the economy, the North American Free Trade Agreement (NAFTA), and later the Whitewater inquiry.

Also, Democratic lawmakers almost immediately started introducing alternative plans to reform health care. The plan faced strong criticism from small-business lobbyists and the Health Insurance Association of America (HIAA). HIAA created the "Harry and Louise" advertisements. The ads "featured a couple agonizing over details of the Clinton plan." For these reasons, President Clinton's attempt to provide Americans with universal health care coverage failed.

"Hillary Care" was never actually debated on its merits. Instead, it was framed politically as big government gone astray and trying to control your life. It was used to brand Clinton as a big government liberal, and along with economic issues, health care would help to flip control of the House of Representatives to Republicans for the first time since 1952 in the midterm elections in 1994.

There was also a new conservative voice rising. Congressman Newt Gingrich of Georgia had created the *Contract with America* as the flag under which Republicans would run for Congress to win the majority. The document turned Republican complaints about Bill Clinton into policy goals and solutions: "The overarching goal of the contract involved cutting taxes, reducing the size of government and reducing government regulations, taking aim at Congress itself, to be more transparent, less corrupt and more open with the public."

This snapshot is a great case study in issues management about how plans fail. Time was not Clinton's friend neither was complexity. Time allowed other issues to percolate to the top, and complexity undermined support. Also, the door was opened for a credible opposition voice, Newt Gingrich, to craft a counter-narrative. Clinton lost the issue and would soon pay the political price for delay and complexity.

The results of the midterm elections were devastating. "Republicans picked up 54 seats in the House of Representatives and 8 seats in the Senate, while also taking control of several governorships and state legislatures. Meanwhile, a handful of prominent Democrats, including House Speaker Tom Foley of Washington and Ways and Means Chairman Dan Rostenkowski of Illinois, suffered unexpected defeats." In January 1995, Newt Gingrich (R-GA) was elected Speaker of the House and Bill Clinton needed to adjust to save his presidency.

The 1994 congressional elections became known as the "Republican Revolution." Republicans acted as if they had a legislative mandate once in power. As reported in JSTOR:

> The Republicans reset the national agenda with bills pushing a tax cut and welfare reform and began nibbling at entitlement programs such as Medicare and Medicaid in the name of fiscal solvency. The Republican majority passed a bill placing constraints on the federal government's ability to force localities to pay for unfunded mandates.

There were several House Republicans who believed in "us versus them" positioning. Congress under Gingrich balkanized the two political parties heralding an end to the form of bipartisanship that had existed in Congress previously.

Clinton accepted responsibility for the defeat. As reported in *the Baltimore Sun*:

> I'm the president. I'm the leader of the efforts that we have made in the last two years, and to whatever extent we didn't do what the people wanted us to do, or they were not aware of what we had done, I must certainly bear my share of responsibility.

The first year of divided government under Clinton was like two ships passing in the night that continued to their separate destinations. Then came the budget. Clinton and Gingrich had major disagreements about how to balance it. This led to a government shutdown for which Republicans would be blamed. The American people were not pleased with the two parties being at war with each other rather than trying to find compromise.

There is an important lesson here about misreading mandates. The American people gave Republicans the majority not to impose their will on Clinton, but to moderate him. Gingrich took the victory to mean that he was empowered to be the "shadow president" and put forth his own agenda for America and force President Clinton to accept it. This came to a head in the budget negotiations and people voiced their dissatisfaction. Clinton would strategically shift and reposition his presidency.

In his State of the Union Address in 1996, Bill Clinton stated: "The era of big government is over." Clinton took the initiative by posing three questions:

> First, how do we make the American Dream of opportunity for all a reality for all Americans who are willing to work for it? Second, how do we preserve our old and enduring values as we move into the future? And third, how do we meet these challenges together, as one America?

It was brilliant. He had repositioned himself as moderate, who wanted bipartisanship, and in the process disarmed his critics. He chided: "Self-reliance and teamwork are not opposing virtues; we must have both."

Clinton then posed six challenges:

1. Cherish our children and strengthen America's families;
2. Provide Americans with the educational opportunities we will all need for this new century;
3. Help every American who is willing to work for it, achieve economic security in this new age;
4. Take our streets back from crime and gangs and drugs;
5. Leave our environment safe and clean for the next generation;
6. Maintain America's leadership in the fight for freedom and peace throughout the world.

The strategy was called triangulation. It was developed for Clinton by his consultant and pollster Dick Morris. It was a "third way" approach that allowed partisans to battle it out on the extremes while Clinton occupied the middle ground. Leading up to the 1996 elections, the "new" Bill Clinton would sign into law Welfare Reform that included a work provision robbing Republicans of an issue. Clinton had the good fortune of governing in sound economic times. He benefited from the "peace dividend" that allowed him to balance the budget. The economy is often the prime element in determining the success of a president. Clinton won reelection in 1996 defeating Senator Bob Dole of Kansas. He would carry 31 states and win 49.2 percent of the popular votes on his way to winning 379 electoral votes. On February 1, 2000, Clinton could boast that he was president during the longest economic expansion in history.

There was also a dark side of the Clinton presidency. As he came into office, there were questions surrounding business deals the Clintons were involved in that were very lucrative, as well as numerous accusations of sexual misconduct when he was governor. These would reach a crescendo when he had an inappropriate relationship with an intern and then lied about it to a grand jury. He would be impeached in the House of Representatives and acquitted in the Senate. All along, Clinton's mantra was that he "wanted to get back to work for the American people," and the American people liked the job he was doing, albeit many had concerns about Bill Clinton's character.

Lessons

At Issue: A president without a clear mandate pursues massive changes to health care and fails, but reassesses, repositions and recovers to salvage his presidency.

Lesson: President Clinton teaches the value of agility in being able to reposition when what you are doing is not working.

1. **Misreading a Mandate**: Clinton was not given a mandate for fundamental change after winning 43 percent of the popular vote in 1992. Compared to presidents like Franklin Roosevelt, Lyndon Johnson, and Ronald Reagan, Clinton had only eked out a victory. In issues management when you misread signals, you can find yourself in trouble. The leader has permission to execute the plan of action that is only as broad as his mandate allows it to be. All leaders must act within assigned parameters that are determined by factors outside of the leader's control. Never assume that permission grants you the ability to carry out your own agenda.

2. **Branding**: Your first move is often your defining move. Clinton won the nomination having solid moderate credentials. His first significant action as president was to reform health care nationally. The message sent was that he would govern as a liberal. This would lose him his crossover appeal and weaken his hand. In issues management, the moves you make early define you and your style of leadership. These definitions will open and close doors to you as they serve to brand your leadership.

3. **Context**: Action always needs context. Surprise is not your friend in issues management. The health care issue was enormously complex and required clear parameters be established for managing it. The Clintons' approach bordered on being an academic exercise. It required too much trust that was not yet earned from the American people. In issues management, context should always precede action especially for enormous undertakings.

4. **Aiming Too High**: Success is built on a solid foundation. It is earned by bringing people along step by step. In issues management you

should guard against showing your hand too early. Clinton had other cards to play. He could have pursued a series of small victories to cement his relationship with Congress and build trust with the American people. Rather than do that, he distanced himself from Congress by going it alone. In issues management, it is not always wise to play your most important card first. It is often better to get a feel for the game and the strategies of others before showing your hand.

5. **Digestive Issues**: Hillary Clinton was a different kind of first lady. Ivy League-educated with a successful career in corporate law before coming to the White House. She and Bill knew she was capable, but the American people did not. This was a new role for a first lady that was far removed from what was expected. It was hard for the American people to get their heads around a "co-presidency" where the first lady would manage major issues. In issues management it is important to read the room. Understand where you are and where the other stakeholders are at all times. You never want to get too far ahead.

6. **Transparency**: Everyone loves a good surprise, but not in issues management. By not keeping people in the loop regarding Hillary's plan suspicion grew. Questions were raised by the press concerning who the members of the task force were. Political enemies began to frame the issue in the worst possible light in the absence of real information. Opponents were given time to plan attacks. In issues management, earning and keeping trust is paramount to achieving success. Hillary had not established anywhere near enough trust to take on a project of this scale in secret.

7. **Complexity Kills**: Health care is a big deal. Any comprehensive plan would have to be very complex. The more complex a solution is, the more targets there are to shoot at. In issues management, big things and little things often merge and are argued as if they are the same. The big picture is lost in translation. Goals and priorities are misaligned. In issues management, a 5-part program approach to a problem will usually work better than a 50-part program. Complex solutions fail because of their weakest links. "Hillary Care" was a

target-rich environment for opponents and a public that was mostly uninformed, meaning that opinion was open to be shaped.

8. **Check With Your Friends**: Before you charge up the hill, turn around to make sure that your army is still behind you. In issues management, time is not always your friend. Perhaps having the plan in place within 100 days would have led to a different result, but the plan was late being completed. During this delay, the political environment had changed, and new priorities developed. By the time it was released, Bill Clinton did not even have all the Democrats with him. Delay had made the political risks greater than the political rewards. In issues management you are always overseeing risk assessment. No environment is stable for very long. As things change, they must be reassessed, and new calculations made about the risks you now face. When the consequences of an action exceed its benefits, then don't pursue the action.

9. **Fracturing**: The sum is not always greater than its parts and progress is incremental. Every election does not call for a second "New Deal." A plan that is overly complex will often be disassembled into more manageable pieces. When an issue fractures, an organization loses its alignment, meaning it is moving in multiple directions rather than toward a shared goal. When smaller bills were introduced to reform health care, "Hillary Care" was doomed. In issues management, your larger initiatives are the most difficult to manage successfully. Timing must be spot on. Fully understanding why people are onboard with your solution is imperative. Monitoring support on an ongoing basis is essential.

10. **Consequences of Failure**: Failure always opens a door to change. In mismanaging health care, Clinton created a "lose-lose" situation wherein he lost credibility and trust, and his party then lost power in Congress in the next election. Being effective at issues management gives a leader a clear path to success, and the benefits can be great. Failure can reveal the flaws a leader has as a manager as well as deficiencies in the leader's ability to create a strategy, organize resources operationally, and execute a plan. It can set an organization back years and deplete its goodwill.

11. **Captain of the Ship**: As president, Clinton was also head of the party, and his actions defined what it meant to be a Democrat during his two terms in office. The party stuck with him until they could not anymore on health care. The issue was so poorly managed that Democrats in Congress risked having to defend big government. They had lost control of the narrative. In issues management, when you are trying to move an organization forward, solve a problem or manage a crisis; you are the captain of the ship. You will have support if you are creating what is perceived as moving toward a "win-win" outcome.

12. **Bouncing Back**: Americans love second chances, where someone learns from failure and is open to new approaches. Getting back into the fight required Clinton to first deal with the consequences of his failure or accept that he would be a one term president. He listened to new voices and accepted new direction. By pursuing a strategy of 'triangulation," Clinton redefined himself on the run. Rather than make his presidency "us versus them" embroiled in constant conflict, he chose to manage issues where opponents fight it out and get bloody, and he would come in and pick up the pieces afterwards and claim victory. It worked.

In 1994, in Clinton's first budget, the national debt stood at $4.7 trillion. In 2001, which would be his last budget, the debt had risen to $5.8 trillion. In eight years, Clinton added only a little more than $1 trillion in new debt. This would not be seen again as we cover the rest of the presidents.

Bill Clinton had a consequential presidency that was conducted in good economic times. He fought small wars abroad, reformed major government programs, and balanced the budget. He was smart and he was above all flexible. He always kept his eye on the ball, working for the American people, no matter how difficult were the issues he faced.

Next up, America elects a former president's son as the political divide grows.

CHAPTER 13

Bush 43—Expanding the Mission

Former U.S. Navy Seal Jocko Willink said it best: "Even the most competent of leaders can be overwhelmed if they try to tackle multiple problems or a number of tasks simultaneously." It is vital in issues management to resolve only the issue for which you created the strategy and not move beyond it. George W. Bush had rallied America behind his War on Terror, but when his initial goal was achieved, he expanded the mission.

In his book, *A Charge to Keep*, George W. Bush wrote about what he learned from his work in the oil business: "I learned how to manage, how to set clear goals and work with people to achieve them."

In 2000, Bush would seek the presidency. He was opposed in the primary election by Sen. John McCain, Alan Keyes, businessman Steve Forbes, conservative Gary Bauer, and Sen. Orrin Hatch. Bush had done his homework and built a solid political organization. He would win the nomination with 1,526 delegates. Sen. John McCain would finish a distant second with 275. As a running mate, Bush selected Dick Cheney, who had both congressional and White House experience.

In the general election, Bush faced Bill Clinton's vice president Al Gore of Tennessee. Gore had to defend the Clinton presidency while presenting his goals for America, but he also was running with a budget surplus that Clinton had achieved in his final year. Although Clinton had not become embroiled in open-ended foreign conflicts, American troops did fight and die in Somalia, about which the book *Blackhawk Down* was written. Bush would say in a campaign debate with Gore that American soldiers should not be used for nation building.

The 2000 election was controversial. On election day, Bush declared himself the winner and Al Gore conceded, but by the end of the night, Gore withdrew his concession and challenged the vote in Florida.

Thus began the Florida recount that would last until the Supreme Court in *Bush v. Gore* on December 11, 2000 declared Bush the winner. Two facts about the election: Bush lost by more than 500,000 in the popular vote count, and he won the electoral vote with 271 votes—one more than the minimum needed.

This was not a good start as Bush's opponents were left with a bitter taste believing that Gore had won and the perception that politics had intervened to elect Bush. On January 6, 2001, 20 Democratic members of the Black Caucus would rise to oppose the Florida results during the Congressional certification of election results.

In his inaugural address, Bush called for unity:

America has never been united by blood or birth or soil. We are bound by ideals that move us beyond our backgrounds, lift us above our interests, and teach us what it means to be citizens. Every child must be taught these principles. Every citizen must uphold them. And every immigrant, by embracing these ideals, makes our country more, not less, American.

Bush intended to focus his presidency on education, but that would not be the case.

On September 11, 2001, the presidency of George W. Bush was changed forever as four commercial jet aircraft were hijacked by terrorists. Two of the jets would destroy the World Trade Center buildings in New York City, one crashed into the Pentagon, and the fourth thundered into a field in Shanksville, Pennsylvania, at over 500 miles per hour. The combined death toll from the attacks was 2,977. Bush's response was immediate and clear—declare war on global terrorism.

Terrorism was not new in the United States, but it was now escalating and becoming more deadly. In 1992, the World Trade Center was bombed and six people were killed. In 1995, a truck bomb in Oklahoma City killed 168. In 2000, the USS Cole was attacked by a suicide bomber killing 17 aboard. All over the world, but especially in the Middle East, terrorism was becoming the weapon of choice to achieve political ends. The massive attack on the U.S. homeland changed Bush's thinking from bringing the culprits to justice using our legal system to finding and killing them using our military and intelligence assets.

Bush would define the enemy as al-Qaeda and its leader as Osama bin Laden. On September 18, 2001, Bush requested an authorization to use force from Congress. His target would be Afghanistan and its Taliban leadership who were supportive of al-Qaeda. On October 7, 2001, the bombing of Afghanistan began. On October 19, 2001, a ground offensive began with our forces allied with anti-Taliban Afghan groups. The Taliban was routed. As reported by the Council of Foreign Relations, "November 14, 2001, the UN Security Council passes Resolution 1378, calling for a 'central role' for the United Nations in establishing a transitional administration and inviting member states to send peacekeeping forces to promote stability and aid delivery." The military operation ended in about five weeks.

On September 22, 2001, George W. Bush's approval rating, according to Gallup, hit 90 percent and for the rest of the year never fell below 86 percent. The War on Terror was very popular with the American people, and Bush was now a wartime president with broad discretionary powers. He would use those powers to pass the Patriot Act in 2001, which applied RICO standards against terrorists and opened the door, some feared, to domestic spying. In 2002, Bush created the Department of Homeland Security that aligned 22 law enforcement and counterintelligence agencies to support the war against terror.

On April 17, 2002, Bush shifted gears when he suggested that the United States should help rebuild Afghanistan along the lines of the Marshall Plan in Europe after World War II. His approval rating was at 77 percent. Billions of dollars began to flow to rebuild Afghanistan. A new "government" was established. It was nation building that would prove to be every bit as difficult as establishing a western style government in South Vietnam four decades earlier.

There was another enemy in proximity—Iraq. Its leader was still Saddam Hussein. He had used chemical weapons in his war against Iran. It was feared he would use them during "Operation Desert Storm" but he did not. Intelligence agencies believed that Saddam had weapons of mass destruction (WMD) that included biological and chemical and that he was attempting to obtain the materials needed to build a nuclear weapon. On March 19, 2003, the United States decided to invade Iraq. The next day a massive air campaign began, followed with ground forces. On May 9, 2003, Saddam Hussein's regime crumbled and the hunt for his key associates began. The faces of those being hunted were represented by a deck of cards, the higher the card, the more important the target. Saddam was the Ace of Spades. On December 14, 2003, Saddam Hussein was captured. On January 14, 2004, the team that was hunting for Saddam's WMDs admitted that none were found. On February 1, 2004, Bush's approval rating dropped to 49 percent.

In his 2004 reelection campaign, Bush would face Sen. John Kerry of Massachusetts. The issue was national security. Kerry was a combat veteran of the Vietnam War. He hit Bush on his reserve service. CBS ran a story using the "Killian Documents" to soil Bush's service record. Dan Rather, the anchor at CBS at the time, ran with the story. The documents were shown to be doctored and not authenticated. Dan Rather lost his news anchor position as a result.

Kerry became an antiwar activist after Vietnam and Bush hit him on his war record and his loyalty to America. Bush called Kerry's "SWIFT Boat" accounts exaggerations and also accused him with making up phony war crimes stories. The strategy worked. Bush would carry more than 51 percent of the vote and win 286 electoral votes.

In his second inaugural address, Bush crystalized his worldview with these few words:

> We are led, by events and common sense, to one conclusion: The survival of liberty in our land increasingly depends on the success of liberty in other lands. The best hope for peace in our world is the expansion of freedom in all the world.

Bush's approval stood at 51 percent. By the end of 2005, it would be at 43 percent. In December 2006, it had dropped to 35 percent. And, by the end of 2008, it had reached 29 percent. Support for his War on Terror had dissipated as nation building became its focus.

Lessons

At Issue: President George W. Bush unleashed a Global War on Terror and allowed circumstance on the ground to alter strategy.

Lesson: President Bush teaches what happens when you set goals and then expand them as new opportunities become available.

1. **Consult History**: Afghanistan is called the "graveyard of empires" because many great nations had tried and failed to bend it to their will. As recently as 1989, Russia retreated having failed to achieve its goals. Tanks, modern armies, and airpower cannot be optimized when fighting in in Afghanistan. History likely would have convinced Bush that the right approach was limited scope engagement rather than nation building. Most issues have a history, and most organizations have a history of issues management. As the leader it is important to study and understand your organization's successes and failures in managing issues and to make the necessary adjustments to strategy and operations before you launch tactics

2. **Nature of the Challenge**: It is also important to fully understand the nature of the challenge you face, because failure to do so can end up costing you time and resources because you have focused on the wrong problem or pursued the wrong strategy. A "War on Terror" is a somewhat amorphous undertaking albeit a good soundbite. Terrorism was global, but this was not a world war. Terrorism is a tactic used by individuals who cannot project power militarily. Terrorism is based on a belief system and cannot be eradicated by killing people, unless you can kill all of them. This puts limitations on power that needs to be incorporated into strategy. Kennedy warned of proxy wars by nuclear powers and Johnson learned the limitations of military power in Vietnam. Bush would have to relearn these lessons fighting terrorism.

3. **Control the Narrative**: The mission going into the war was clear: We were going to get the people who killed Americans on 9/11 and bring them to justice. This was the bargain Bush made with the American people, who would accept the killing, imprisoning, and disbanding terror operations globally to stop terrorist attacks. The goal was simple: Make sure this does not happen again. The issues management problem is when victory is elusive, the narrative becomes more difficult to control, and it must be adjusted to conform with new realities

on the ground. In issues management, when you must change the narrative, it is time to assess the strategy, because your objectives have likely changed. Applying the same narrative to new situations does not always work, and you may find yourself in territory you cannot defend and from which you cannot accomplish objectives.

4. **Simple Solutions**: Initial thinking seemed to be that if we toppled the government that harbored the terrorists and killed the leader, the problem would be solved. There was nothing simple about the challenge of fighting terrorism. It flourished in some of the poorest and most uncivilized, by western standards, regions of the world. In issues management, a solution that is too simple often gives birth to an extremely complex problem. In the case of Afghanistan, it led to nation building to create a western-style democracy in a land ruled by warring tribes for centuries.

5. **Create Metrics**: The metric often used in measuring the success of the War on Terror is the number of days it has been since terrorists attacked the homeland. The assumption is that no attacks on the homeland directly equated to successful operations. Only to a point. In issues management having benchmarks is important. Picking reliable metrics can be a great asset in maintaining focus, directing resources, and evaluating success, but they require very thoughtful planning and an honest assessment when creating them. Bad metrics can often create false positive results that give the impression that progress is greater than it is.

6. **Take the Win**: Both the Taliban government in Afghanistan and the government of Saddam Hussein in Iraq fell in a matter of months after our military assault began. At this point our military had done its job. Rather than declaring victory, Bush redefined the mission to nation building. In issues management, achieving your initial objective is the end point. The question confronting leaders, and it is one of the most difficult in issues management, is when and how you accept victory. President Roosevelt could not stop reforming and President Johnson could not stop trying to win an unwinnable war. Now George Bush suffered the same fate. because he was unwilling to move on.

7. **Scale Creep**: The thing about success is that you want more of it. The "War on Terror" was very popular with the American people and

Bush's popularity grew. A common mistake in issues management is when something works once it should be tried again even when the problem is not the same. The reason for invading Afghanistan was not the same as invading Iraq. In issues management, there is the temptation to do more than is in the plan. Go beyond your mandate to get more results. This is unwise because when you move beyond your primary mission, the situation is rarely the same. The strategy that worked so well and was so clear to solve one issue fails to achieve the desired result on the next issue.

8. **Break It—Fix It**: In war you break things and kill people. After that is done, then the nature of war changes to fix things and help people. The large military operations in the nations of Afghanistan and Iraq ended quickly and the humanitarian needs were massive in their wake. In issues management, there are often relationships that need to be mended and friendships reestablished after the engagement ends. If you accept credit, then you also accept accountability to repair what you have broken. If you ask for sacrifice, then you must be willing to pay it back in kind.

9. **Failure**: In war there is always collateral damage. In this war, it was Abu Ghraib where war prisoners were abused by the guards. The longer you are in conflict mode, then the more likely it is that something bad will happen, and when it does, it can undermine the narrative. A rule of successful issues management is success needs to outpace failure, because failure always trumps success in public opinion. The fighter is a champion until he loses. Failures are like flat tires on a road trip. They take time to fix and delay getting to where you are going. Strategy needs to be clear and execution should be efficient.

10. **Too Deep**: You reach a point where there is no clear way to exit your current position. Events now are in control of your strategy. This is the point where the "bang for your buck" is greatly diminished. On December 18, 2011, our final troops were withdrawn from Iraq. On August 30, 2021, the United States completed its final withdrawal from Afghanistan. You can manage issues forever if that is what you choose to do with your time and resources. George H.W. Bush ended the First Gulf War because his stated objective was achieved. The objectives of George W. Bush were more ill-defined,

so he ended up with a growing divide between the victory he first claimed and the victory he ended up pursuing. In the end there was nothing clear or attainable left on the table.

George W. Bush's presidency was bookended by crisis. He pursued his "War on Terror" with a sense of omnipotence, seemingly pursuing goals that were more theoretical than practical. In his second crisis, banking and real estate, he was much humbler. He used the power and resources of the federal government to achieve a clear objective. Many believe that his decisive actions saved the United States from entering another depression. In any case, his actions provided his successor with a more stable financial environment in which to begin his presidency.

Next up Barack Obama and health care achieved.

CHAPTER 14

Obama—Learning From History

Otto von Bismarck said: "Fools say that they learn by experience. I prefer to profit by others experience." In issues management you don't need to constantly reinvent the wheel. Build on past successes and avoid the mistakes made by others. Barack Obama learned from the failure of Hillary Clinton's health care initiative to craft and pass Obamacare into law.

Barack Obama's ascendancy to the presidency was meteoric. He served as a state senator in Illinois beginning in 1996 and was elected to the U.S. Senate in 2004. That year, like Bill Clinton before him, he gave a speech at the Democratic National Convention. His gift for public speaking was extraordinary, and the speech was a big hit and provided him with a platform from which to rise within the Democratic Party.

The New York Times reported on his tenure in the U.S. Senate, writing: "They were the two competing elements in Mr. Obama's time in the Senate: his megawatt celebrity and the realities of the job he was elected to do." Obama was 99th in seniority and in the minority party while in the Senate, but Obama was ambitious and charismatic. It was more his celebrity than his accomplishments that drove his appeal. He was more of a rock star than a master legislator in the mold of Lyndon Johnson.

Before the end of this first term in the Senate, Obama saw an opportunity and he took it. On February 10, 2007, in Springfield, Missouri, he announced his candidacy for the presidency by stating:

> You ... came here because you believe in what this country can
> be. In the face of war, you believe there can be peace. In the face
> of despair, you believe there can be hope. In the face of a politics
> that shut you out, that's told you to settle, that's divided us for too

long, you believe that we can be one people, reaching for what's possible, building that more perfect union.

Then, he issued a generational challenge:

Let's be the generation that ends poverty in America … And let's be the generation that finally, after all these years, tackles our health care crisis … Let's be the generation that finally frees America from the tyranny of oil … Most of all, let's be the generation that never forgets what happened on that September day and confront the terrorists with everything we've got.

Obama was a unique candidate: biracial, raised by a single mother, and Ivy League educated. He was also an enigma. Many said he was like a mirror who could be whoever you wanted to see. Then Senator Joe Biden would say this about Obama: "I mean, you got the first mainstream African-American who is articulate and bright and clean and a nice-looking guy."

Obama's main competition for the nomination was former First Lady and now senator from New York, Hillary Clinton. It was a tough primary that went down to the wire. Obama would be the nominee. He selected Senator Joe Biden of Delaware as his running mate. On the Republican side, Senator John McCain carried the day besting Gov. Mike Huckabee of Arkansas among others. McCain selected Gov. Sarah Palin of Alaska to fill out the ticket.

The issues in the campaign included the war in Iraq and the surge of troops President Bush had ordered to regain the initiative. Also, Bush had become very unpopular with missteps in managing Hurricane Katrina among other matters. Age was on the table as this was one of the obvious contrasts for the youthful Obama to exploit, as was the economy that took a tremendous hit in September with the banking crisis. Lastly, there was health care. McCain supported a free-market approach, while Obama called for universal health care.

There were two factors that turned this race in Obama's favor. The first was Sarah Palin. She was attractive and witty with a down-home style, but she was not well-versed on the issues. Then there was social media.

It was a new phenomenon in 2008, and the Obama campaign would be the first to exploit its potential to touch people, keep them informed, listen to their concerns, create enthusiasm, stay ahead of media stories and drive voter turnout.

Obama would win by 10 million votes and secure 365 electoral votes. America had elected its first Black president. He would enter office a blank slate.

In his first inaugural address, Obama called for collective action:

> But we have always understood that when times change, so must we; that fidelity to our founding principles requires new responses to new challenges; that preserving our individual freedoms requires collective action. For the American people can no more meet the demands of today's world by acting alone than American soldiers could have met the forces of fascism or communism with muskets and militias.

The theme of his campaign was "Hope and Change," but he painted what he planned to do in broad and opaque brushstrokes.

On October 9, 2009, Obama would be awarded the Nobel Peace Prize for "his extraordinary efforts to strengthen international diplomacy and cooperation between peoples." What concretely had he done? Arguable nothing, but that was the Obama mystique where intentions were rewarded as if they are actions. It mattered more what he said than what he did in a lot of instances. It was his gift and he used it to his advantage.

As president, Obama was aloof, noncommittal, above it all, and mostly alone. *The New York Times* story printed on August 18, 2014, summarized a meeting in the Oval Office with both Senate and House leaders concerning the "unraveling situation in Iraq." At the meeting, Democratic leader Harry Reid and Republican leader Mitch McConnell moved to the topic of Republicans' failure to move Obama judge appointments through the confirmation process. Reid expected Obama to take his side and urge McConnell to act. Instead, Obama said: "You and Mitch work it out," ending the discussion.

On August 19, 2014, the story "A Brief History of President Obama Not Having Any Friends" was published in *The Atlantic*. The condensed version is captured in the piece by this quote: "Over the years dozens of stories have described the relationship between a president who wants to be 'above it all' and members of Congress who want the president to pose for photos they can hang on their walls."

In a piece in *Politico*, it was cited that: "When Democratic lawmakers gather in private, their complaints about Obama's perennial lack of outreach to them are frequent and sustained." *The New Yorker* piece recounted Obama's snub of George Soros for which "he felt hurt." Another *The New York Times* article in 2012 spoke to his relationship-building skills, "His relationship with most Democratic members of Congress lies somewhere between correct and cold. They believe that personal political loyalties are not an Obama priority." Scott Wilson, writing in *The Washington Post*, provided this observation of Obama's style of governing: "His relationship with Democrats on Capitol Hill is frosty, to be generous," Wilson continued, "Personal lobbying on behalf of legislation? He prefers to leave that to Vice President Biden, an old-school political charmer."

When Obama was sworn-in as president in 2009, he had 56 Democrats in the U.S. Senate; the number would grow to 60 senators and 255 in the House of Representatives. These were solid majorities that positioned Obama to take big political risks if he chose to take them. The 60 votes in the Senate made any bills taken up in the Senate filibuster-proof. In the House, Obama had Speaker Nancy Pelosi (D-CA), who was known for her ability to get the votes needed to pass legislation. This was an ideal moment to push through a big agenda item—health care reform.

Many think that the Affordable Care Act, known as Obamacare, was just "Hillary Care" called by another name. A Forbes analysis of the bill found: "In 2009, when the Affordable Care Act was written by Congress, the health insurance industry, led by America's Health Insurance Plans, supported the legislation," and concluded, "The failure of Hillary and Bill Clinton to get the insurance industry on board for the Clinton 'Health Security Act' was something that Democrats and the Obama administration learned from."

As reported in *The New York Times*, Obamacare was an extension of a Republican idea:

The concept that people should be required to buy health coverage was fleshed out more than two decades ago by a number of conservative economists, embraced by scholars at conservative research groups, including the Heritage Foundation and the American Enterprise Institute, and championed, for a time, by Republicans in the Senate.

This provided great political positioning for the Democrats because the issue could fit with both political philosophies. Checkmate!

When the legislation was signed into law in March 2010, according to NBC polling, 48 percent of Americans thought it was a bad idea and 36 percent thought it was a good idea. In January 2017, seven years later, those who thought it was a good idea stood at 45 percent and those who thought it was a bad idea at 41 percent.

In 2017, *The New York Times* reported that the debate on Obamacare had changed citing: "There is a shifting public focus away from what is wrong with the Affordable Care Act to a world where 21 million people could lose coverage," said Robert Blendon, a professor of health policy and political analysis at Harvard. Blendon added: "The Affordable Care Act may not be more popular, but the implications of repeal are shifting people to a less negative stand on the law."

Obamacare gave Republicans an issue. In 2010, in a special election to fill the seat of the late senator Edward M. "Ted" Kennedy of Massachusetts, Republican Scott Brown ran for and won the seat in this "deep blue" state. His issue was repeal of Obamacare. Republicans put forth at least 16 plans to repeal or replace Obamacare since its passage. They all failed.

In the 2010 midterms, Republicans would pick up five seats in the U.S. Senate and regain the majority in the House of Representatives. The new Speaker of the House was John Boehner. Although power shifted because of the Obamacare issue, Republicans were savvy enough politically to realize that the gap between a political mandate and creating a viable legislative alternative that could pass in Congress was wide. There would be no repeal of Obamacare. Shared power would continue after the 2012 elections. In 2014, Republicans would regain control of the Senate and maintain control of the House of Representatives. Obama was personally popular, but his popularity never translated to other Democrats.

There is a good lesson here in issues management about knowing the kind of mandate you are given. The way in which Obamacare was enacted created trust issues with the electorate. There were several backroom deals cut to get votes. In 2010, Republicans were given a political mandate to make sure that the Democrats did not go any further down the road to controlling health care rather than a mandate to repeal it. Their mandate really was to guard the line and they understood it.

There is also a lesson here on shifting loyalties. Every action you take impacts individuals and groups in separate ways. The longer you manage an issue, the more shifts in support you are likely to see. This is one reason why your actions need to be focused and targeted. Protracted issues management can result in the loss of key support as we saw when Bill Clinton presented health care reform.

Crisis comes to you, but issues are prioritized for management. Was President Obama the driving force behind Obamacare? It could be argued that the real drivers of the bill were Speaker Nancy Pelosi and Senate Majority Leader Harry Reid. Obama would own the bill and pay the price by having his approval ratings fall, but he was not on the ballot in 2010. The price would be paid by House and Senate members and by Nancy Pelosi, who lost her Speakership. So, what can we learn from the passage of Obamacare?

Lessons

At Issue: President Barack Obama, with solid majorities in both houses of Congress, had the opportunity to pass health care which was the final piece of the "New Deal."

Lesson: President Obama teaches us the value of learning from the mistakes of the past and using this knowledge to successfully manage complex issues going forward.

1. **Frame the Problem:** Health insurance was traditionally delivered by employers in the United States. This created gaps for those transitioning in the workforce and those who had lost their jobs. According to Pew Research, health insurance was not among the top five issues the American people cared about in 2010: Economy, Jobs, Terrorism, Social Security, and Medicare were identified. In fact, health insurance was rated 12th in the poll. In issues management, choosing an issue that is not perceived as a pressing problem provides

the benefit of being able to frame it in your terms before you focus attention on it. It also carries the cost of having to overcome initial resistance because it is not a top priority.

2. **Play Your Hand**: Obama had Nancy Pelosi running the House of Representatives. She was the consummate operative in this situation. She was very adept at moving legislation. In the Senate there were 60 Democrats. This rendered Republican opposition futile. In issues management, having great people at the operational level is a tremendous asset. Also, having enough political capital and goodwill to render opposition impotent is a strong position from which to launch a new and controversial program. Solid positioning, in terms of your ability to get the results you desire, is a tremendous asset in managing issues. Also, having knowledgeable people in place to monitor progress and shifts in support can prove to be invaluable in managing complex issues.

3. **Learn From Others**: Hillary Clinton had failed to pass her health care bill in 1993. This could be viewed as defeat or simply as a lesson to learn. In any setback, always do an after-action report to understand what factors precipitated failure. No plan is 100 percent right or wrong. There are good things in most plans that can be incorporated into the next plan as well as "green lights – red lights" that warn of things to avoid next time. From the start, legislative leaders knew the mistakes Hillary Clinton had made in launching her plan, and they would not repeat them when given a second bite of the apple. Never start a project with a blank sheet of paper. Know what worked in the past and what failed and incorporate both into your new plan.

4. **Get Buy-in**: Endorsements are a slippery slope in issues management. It is often assumed that getting people on board gives an effort gravitas. The real task is making sure the right people are on board. These are the people who can advance your issue. With Obamacare, the right people were the health insurers. They provided the image of cooperation and the imprimatur that the insurers, whom the American people trusted, were looking out for their interests. The simple rule for endorsements is accept anyone with influence who agrees with your approach. It is like having an expert witness at a trial. The other lesson here is muting objections before they are

stated. This is part of a good planning process. Reaching out early to get the insurers involved was likely the smartest move made.

5. **Control the Noise**: "Hillary Care" was opposed by the insurance industry, and they ran ads to help defeat it. This was the experts saying this was not a good bill. In a way they were the voice of the American people in that fight. Ads would be run against Obamacare only after the bill was passed and it became a ripe political issue. Most of the ads were run by conservative groups supporting candidates who had promised to repeal and replace Obamacare. Political ads are political. Conservative ads have an agenda. In issues management, your communications program should contain components focused on controlling the noise. This means controlling misinformation and mischaracterization. A lot of this is achieved by getting the buy-in we talked about earlier. When managing an issue effectively, know who are your friends, enemies, fence sitters and those who are persuadable and build a plan for each category.

6. **Keep It Simple**: The Clinton proposal focused on reforming the health care system in America. Obamacare focused on reforming how Americans buy health insurance. On the floor of the Senate, during the debate on the Clinton plan, Senator Arlen Specter (R-PA) prepared a flowchart depicting the plan. It was extremely complicated and gave senators pause to vote for something they would have a challenging time explaining back home. Obamacare had a more limited focus. It was not simple but also not overly complex. In issues management, you don't want to reinvent the wheel with each issue you address. Often a problem has many parts. It is better to solve many small problems than to fail at trying to solve one big one.

7. **Fair Hearing**: Obamacare was debated for 25 consecutive days in Congress. The bottom line was that Republicans did not have the votes to stop it. When you hold all the cards, it is always good practice to allow those opposed to your plan to have their say before you have your way. On November 7, 2009, Nancy Pelosi delivered 220 votes to pass Obamacare. If she had 218 votes, then she did not have to make any concessions to anyone who opposed the bill. In issues management, sometimes your entire team cannot be with you. As long as you have the votes you need, it is usually wise to not force

them take an uncomfortable position. Pelosi recognized that some of her more conservative members could not support the bill.

8. **Maintain Transparency**: When Bill Clinton appointed Hillary Clinton to craft a health care plan for America, she instinctively created a secret committee. The names of its members were not initially released. There was no such committee created for Obamacare. Yes, it relied on experts, but the bill was an action of Congress that would have an open debate. In issues management don't spring surprises. Keep as much as possible transparent. What cannot be done transparently, try to report out quickly. Plans that are created in secret lose a high degree of credibility and can quickly lose support. Surprises are rarely positive in issues management.

9. **Remove Scary**: Change is always a tricky thing for the public to accept, so you have to provide assurances along the way. Even though Obamacare was a partisan undertaking, Democrats worked with health insurers to create it, and they had plenty of floor debate, so it was perceived to be a fair process. When managing issues, it is important to understand what makes people uncomfortable because discomfort fast tracks opposition and dampens support. When dealing with fundamental change, provide as much comfort as possible by assuring people that the issue has been fully vetted.

10. **Cover**: The bill was signed in March 2010, which was an election year for Congress. The 219 Democrats in the House who voted for the bill (there was one Republican vote) had to stand for reelection with full responsibility for their vote but nothing tangible to show their voters. The Obamacare website would not be launched until October 1, 2013. They had to run with all the costs and none of the benefits. In issues management, tactics can outdistance results and messaging. Republicans, in 2010, had a clear field to focus on other issues like the economy, deficit, illegal immigration, energy, Obama's troop surge, and terrorism while also attacking Democrats on Obamacare—the issue they alone owned. Republicans would regain control of the House. Obamacare would be reframed several years later as support galvanized around not repealing it, because too many people would be hurt. Issue evolution happens over time, and often you cannot control the timing. Initially, there will

be resistance, so education is particularly important. There is also the risk of leaving your supporters high and dry by moving on to other issues after they have gone to bat for you. Time and resources should be made available to help them through this process. The project will often need to continue after the goal has been achieved. Be there for those who helped after the issue is settled. That way you will have allies going forward to help with the next issue.

When Obama ran for reelection in 2012, Vice President Joe Biden summed up his first term with this simple phrase: "Osama Bin Laden is dead; General Motors is alive." This is telling for an administration that had enacted and signed into law Obamacare. In the main, President Obama stayed above the fray. He earned the moniker: "No drama Obama." But the record is not complete. *Politico* wrote this about his leadership on civil rights:

> Lyndon B. Johnson rallied public opinion against disenfranchisement a half-century ago. When he announced the proposal that became the Voting Rights Act, he invoked the anthem of the civil rights movement: "We Shall Overcome." Why can't Obama muster some passion of his own? He has repeatedly lauded the heroics of Rep. John Lewis and the other activists who dramatized the need for legislation in the 1960s. Yet today, with that same legislation confronting new perils, the president remains quiet.

That is not who Barack Obama is.

This is too much to lay at the feet of one man, but issues are choices, and he never chose to be "all in" on the one issue that likely would have landed him on Mt. Rushmore—race in America.

Next up is Donald J. Trump and the noise that derailed his presidency.

CHAPTER 15

Trump—Self-Fulfilling Prophecy

Again, I turn to Winston Churchill to frame this chapter, "You have enemies? Good. It means you stood up for something, sometime in your life." In issues management there is always another point of view. Standing your ground is mostly a good thing if you realize that your actions can also serve to unite your opposition. Donald J. Trump did not have opponents as much as he did enemies, and as a result, he always ran the risk of becoming the person his enemies said he was in the minds of the American people.

Trump's career in politics started with an escalator ride down to the ground floor at Trump Tower in New York City on June 15, 2015. Joining him was his wife, Melania. In his announcement, he chose immigration to frame his campaign saying:

> When Mexico sends its people, they're not sending their best. They're sending people that have lots of problems, and they're bringing those problems with us (sic). They're bringing drugs, they're bringing crime, they're rapists. And some, I assume, are good people.

Many reporters were shocked by his bluntness, but it would be the tone of his presidency: tell it how you see it, let the chips fall where they may, don't worry about the feelings of others, and never apologize for something you said.

Donald John Trump is a son of New York City. He was born in the borough of Queens. His father was highly successful in real estate. He attended military school in New York and initially Fordham University. He transferred to the University of Pennsylvania, where he graduated from the prestigious Wharton School of Business. He then took over his father's business, renamed it the Trump Organization, and became a billionaire by building and managing luxury properties, golf resorts, and hotels around the world.

Trump is a celebrity. His exploits were often reported on "Page Six" of the *New York Post*. He dated glamorous women. Lived a jet set lifestyle. Elevated himself to a brand that signified luxury and status. As an author who wrote about his own success. His book: *Trump: The Art of the Deal*, "reached number one on The New York Times Best Seller list, stayed there for 13 weeks." He hosted "The Apprentice" that aired between 2004 and 2017. The show focused on a group of contestants being divided into teams to work on business focused tasks. At the end of each episode, one contestant would be let go using Trump's classic pronouncement: "You're Fired." The last person standing would become the apprentice and go to work on one of Trump's projects. During the program's run, Trump would earn $214 million.

Trump was married three times and is the father of five children. His residence was the penthouse in Trump Tower on Fifth Avenue in Manhattan. That is where he came down the escalator to start his new career in politics.

The presidency was open in 2016, and 17 Republicans competed for the nomination in the primary. Trump exhibited remarkable appeal as a first-time candidate running for the highest office in the land. Trump finished a surprising second to Sen. Ted Cruz in the Iowa caucuses and would win in New Hampshire. Better known candidates, including John Ellis "JEB" Bush, former two-term governor of Florida, son of a former president, and brother to another, would not survive the primary process against Trump, who would secure the nomination on May 3, 2016.

On the Democratic side, the nomination was also contested. Hillary Clinton, who had been First Lady, senator from New York, and Secretary of State under President Obama, was the front runner. She received a surprising challenge from Senator Bernie Sanders (I-VT) who is a Democratic-Socialist. His strength in the Democratic primaries surprised many. Hillary would win the first contest, the Iowa caucuses, by only two-tenths of one point. Sanders would win New Hampshire, but Clinton would go on to win 54 percent of the pledged delegates and carry a whopping 94 percent of superdelegates to secure the nomination.

During the primary process, Trump had shown unexpected strength and Clinton unanticipated weakness. The race for the White House was on.

Despite being a billionaire, Trump had a surprising appeal to the working class. His message was "Make America Great Again," and his theme was "America First." His appeal was to middle America, which Trump believed had been forgotten by the powerful elites in Washington. Trump was a conservative populist at his core and a pragmatist in his actions.

Few thought that Trump could win the general election, but he was a ratings sensation. He received billions of dollars in free media coverage as a result. Many in the press saw Trump as hell-bent on destroying the new global order. They often branded his words and policies as nativist, isolationist, racist, and protectionist. This branding was not effectively managed during the campaign and would dominate Trump's presidency as well as negatively impact public opinion of him.

In September, Hillary Clinton was tripped up when documents were released showing she used a personal e-mail address to conduct Department of State business. She then deleted tens of thousands of her e-mails, saying they were personal. The computers that contained the information were destroyed and their contents erased. Also, Hillary was taped at an event calling Trump's supporters "deplorables" and accusing them of being "racist, sexist, homophobic, xenophobic, Islamophobic—you name it."

On October 7, 2016, the Billy Bush audio tape was released in which Trump was heard using the foulest of language to sexualize women. He was roundly condemned by many in the Republican establishment who believed this would end his campaign. His campaign called it a private matter that happened a long time ago. He did not deny the report was true. He survived an issue that would have upended most campaigns.

There was one more shoe to drop in the campaign. In the months leading up to the election. a document called the "Steele Dossier" was released. In the dossier, which was prepared by a former British spy named Christopher Steele, Trump was accused of colluding with the Russian government as well as performing several untoward activities that the Russians could use to blackmail him were he to become president.

Using something called "circular reporting," the dossier got into the mainstream media and was referred to several investigative agencies of government creating a cloud of suspicion around Trump that would hound him for most of his presidency. Circular reporting is when one source reports an unfounded rumor and then other sources report on the reporting of the rumor as if it were factual.

On election night, Trump won states that most Republicans do not ordinarily win, including Pennsylvania, Michigan, and Wisconsin. The media was shocked as polling had indicated a comfortable victory for Hillary Clinton. In the SHOWTIME documentary that chronicled the campaign, "Trumped: Inside the Greatest Political Upset of All Time," Mark Halperin, John Heilemann, and Mark McKinnon followed the evolution of Donald Trump as a candidate. On election night, Halperin and Heilemann were in New York City making the rounds of the talk shows, assuming a victory for Hillary Clinton. As the night wore on, their certainty began to erode, and then it disappeared. Heilemann was speechless as he went to the nearly empty Hillary campaign headquarters late in the evening. There would be no concession speech from the candidate because she had not prepared one. The polls were wrong. The pundits missed it. Trump was president. The most improbable man ever elected president was now going to lead the United States. But it was a fractured nation, and the chasm would only grow wider with each passing year.

In his inaugural address, Trump was on message:

> For too long, a small group in our nation's capital has reaped the rewards of government, while the people have borne the cost. Washington flourished, but the people did not share in its wealth. Politicians prospered, but the jobs left, and the factories closed. The establishment protected itself, but not the citizens of our country. Their victories have not been your victories. Their triumphs have not been your triumphs, and while they celebrated in our nation's capital, there was little to celebrate for struggling families across our land. That all changes, starting right here and right now, because this moment is your moment.

Yet, two other events, one that day and the one next day would become a metaphor for the Trump presidency. In Washington DC, there were protests that turned violent. NBC News reported that 217 people were arrested. In the riot, "Six police officers suffered minor injuries when protesters flung bricks, trash cans and other objects, and ignited small fires." The protesters carried signs that read "Not my president," "No Islamophobia," and "Black Lives Matter." Property was destroyed and cars were burned.

The next day was the Women's March on Washington. It was an event organized on social media in response to the "Billy Bush tape" that was released during the campaign.

> The idea of the Women's March began on the social networking website Facebook the day after the election, when a Hawaii woman named Teresa Shook voiced her opinion that a pro-woman march was needed as a reaction to Trump's victory.

At the event, entertainer Madonna said that she "thought an awful lot about blowing up the White House" and continued that it "took this horrific moment of darkness to wake us the f–k up." She told the crowd: "It seems as though we had all slipped into a false sense of comfort, that justice would prevail and that good would win in the end." She concluded: "Well, good did not win this election. But good will win in the end." Trump's political opponents had declared war on his presidency.

According to Gallup, Trump's presidency began with a 45 percent approval rating. During his entire term, Trump would never attain 50 percent approval. With all the other presidents, issues and events drove approval up or down. With Trump, it never mattered to about half of America what he achieved in domestic or foreign policy or whether the economy was booming or heading into a depression. With Trump, all that mattered to his opponents was Trump.

America had changed leading into the Trump presidency. Obama was able to keep a lid on things during his two terms because, most of the time, he chose not to make waves. He was not confrontational. He earned good press. He achieved his great political victory early in his presidency.

He usually left the heavy political lifting and the dirty work for others to do. He did not have a lot of pesky scandals or congressional investigations to deal with over his eight years in office. There was criticism, but nothing seemed to stick.

Trump entered office in 2017 under a cloud of suspicion created by the Steele Dossier. The narrative that Trump was Putin's puppet hung over his presidency like a dark cloud. Even in 2021, the theory was still being advanced. *The Guardian* wrote a piece titled "'The perfect target': Russia cultivated Trump as asset for 40 years—ex-KGB spy." *The New York Times Magazine* piece carried this title: "An Ex-KGB Agent Says Trump Was a Russian Asset Since 1987. Does It Matter?" In 2023, the report filed by special prosecutor John Durham concluded the entire matter of "Russiagate" was made up, and that several law enforcement institutions of government had failed. It went largely unreported in the media.

Trump also did himself no favors. He seemed determined to chime in on every issue and dispute every criticism. His weapon of choice was the social media platform, Twitter. All hours of the day and night, he would "tweet" his criticisms of people and frame events and tout his policies and accomplishments. On many occasions, Trump would "bury the lede" on successful initiatives with ill-timed tweets. On many newscasts, the reporting was on Trump's tweet and not about an issue he was managing. He also declared war on the press, defining left leaning media as "fake news."

It is important here to try to understand what factors contributed to creating the political divide. At the macro level, there were several trends that changed how information flowed in America. In 2017, there were about 27 million active daily users of Twitter in the United States. This number would grow to 40 million during Trump's presidency.

The news business had been radically transformed by social media. Newspapers were now dependent on subscribers for revenue. Keeping subscribers happy meant feeding them the news they wanted to read and the commentary with which they agreed. *The New York Times* veered more left, while *The Wall Street Journal* provided more conservative commentary. Lastly, cable news outlets took sides to boost ratings. Fox News provided Trump with a mostly unfiltered outlet, while MSNBC and CNN gave voice to Trump's opponents.

The impact of social media in changing our society cannot be stressed enough. In an opinion piece in *The New York Times* in 2018 titled "Social media is making us dumber," Jesse Singal wrote: "What social media is doing is slicing the salami thinner and thinner, as it were, making it harder even for people who are otherwise in general ideological agreement to agree on basic facts about news events."

What social media did was take complex issues and break them down into soundbites, chants, and slogans. It also stifled the willingness to debate issues by branding any person who did not tow the approved line as racist, sexist, homophobic, fascist, Nazi, or even Hitler reincarnate. Social media helped to create virtual mobs that policed platforms to find people, groups, organizations, and businesses that warranted social isolation by being silenced. This would become known as "cancel culture." Through social media, a cultural orthodoxy was created that had one set of beliefs that almost rose to the level of religion. Those who questioned those beliefs were considered heretic and branded as such. For example, anyone who did not totally accept the prescribed beliefs about climate change was branded as a "climate denier."

Forgiveness and second chances were the first victims of the rise of social media. Alexi McCammond had worked her entire career to be in the right position to be hired by *Teen Vogue* as editor. Her career was short lived. She "drew complaints" because of perceived racist and homophobic tweets she had posted a decade ago. *The New York Times* reported her statement in which she wrote that her "past tweets have overshadowed the work I've done to highlight the people and issues that I care about." It did not matter. McCannond's boss knew the consequences of defending her could ruin the brand. McCammond was only 27 years old. The mob won.

The epithets leveled against Trump provided a lot of leeway for Trump's opponents to do or say anything if it comported with the anti-Trump narrative. Many vocal Trump opponents today would be hard-pressed to name five issues Trump managed as president. That is because Trump was always the issue and not his policies.

Despite deep divisions in America, pre-Covid-19, the country was doing quite well. The middle class enjoyed higher wages, inflation was low, economic growth was robust, minorities were doing better economically, the border was secure, and the world was at peace. Trump was well-positioned for reelection in 2020.

Then on January 20, 2020, "CDC confirms the first U.S. laboratory-confirmed case of COVID-19 in the U.S. from samples taken on January 18 in Washington state." This was a novel corona virus that was first detected in Wuhan, China, a month before. Trump would be thrust into managing a full-blown crisis.

Trump's initial response in January 2020 was to say: "We have it totally under control. It's one person coming in from China. It's going to be just fine." About a week later, Trump adviser Peter Navarro wrote this in a memo to him:

> The lack of immune protection or an existing cure or vaccine would leave Americans defenseless in the case of a full-blown coronavirus outbreak on US soil … This lack of protection elevates the risk of the coronavirus evolving into a full-blown pandemic, imperiling the lives of millions of Americans.

Throughout most of the month of February 2020, Trump repeated that the virus was under control and would go away. The reality was the United States was not ready for a pandemic. We lacked basic supplies for hospitals, including masks, protective gear, and ventilators. There were no reliable tests for Covid-19. Basic medicines were no longer made in America. Most importantly, we had no vaccines or therapeutics with which to treat the disease.

The Covid-19 timeline is a good example of how an issue grows into a crisis. On March 5, 2020, there were a total of 11 deaths reported, and Trump was still urging calm. Trump's initial strategy, as he would tell Bob Woodward, was always to play the virus down. On March 15, 2020, Trump announced "15 days to slow the spread." It was sold as a temporary shutdown of the economy. By late March, Trump's position changed to we can't have the cure be worse than the disease itself. Trump was also saying that he inherited a mess, meaning that the pantry was bare and we were not prepared for a full-blown pandemic.

In early spring 2020, the world shut down. The initial strategy was to isolate, social distance and wear a mask. Nations closed. States closed.

Businesses closed. Schools closed. Work became remote. Offices and shelves emptied.

As an issues manager, Trump focused on creating more PPE, building more ventilators, sending hospital ships to cities in crises, using the Army Corps of Engineers to build makeshift hospitals, and creating new vaccines. His vaccine development plan was called "Operation Warp Speed." Trump's focus was to lower regulatory barriers to vaccine development, align government agencies to support vaccine approval, use federal power to order private businesses to produce needed products, speed up the approval process, limit liability for the pharmaceutical companies, and invest federal funds in selected pharma companies to offset expenses and financial risk.

Trump was uniquely positioned to run this operation as president. He had spent his life building complex projects with a lot of moving parts and making deals with vendors. He was skilled at multitasking and delegating. The American people were scared. They did not understand the virus and needed assurances that there was light at the end of the tunnel. Trump decided to do daily briefings.

At the briefings were medical professionals who comprised his Covid Response Team. Their job was to track the virus. He would also bring in CEOs to discuss vaccine development and heads of other agencies as needed. On center stage was Trump. On April 23, 2000, Trump thought out loud about the role he thought disinfectants could play in tackling an infection caused by the virus. It was reported that Trump was telling Americans to drink bleach. Trump rambled on at most of the briefings and often got into verbal spats with the press and arguments with his own staff. He stopped the briefings for months only to restart them with him playing less of a primary role.

The political divide manifested itself in the debate about therapeutics that included monoclonal antibodies, ivermectin, remdesivir, paxlovid, fluvaximine, and others. They would become mostly ignored by Trump opponents and promoted in "red states" like Florida. The medical community also split over treatments and the benefits of masks and shutdowns. Social media would shut down a lot of this debate where the opinions of world renown scientists were being dismissed out of hand.

In November 2020, Trump appointed Army Gen. Gustave F. Perna, an expert in logistics, to develop a distribution plan for vaccines. The plan was doable. On December 13, 2020, the first vaccine was administered in the United States.

It never mattered to about half of America what Trump accomplished by bringing vaccines to market in just eight months. The only thing that ever mattered to them was getting rid of Trump. On November 3, 2020, 81 million Americans voted for Joe Biden to make that happen.

Trump had become the person his enemies always said he was during the Covid-19 press conferences.

Lessons

At Issue: President Donald Trump assumes the chief executive role to create and implement a plan to develop, distribute, and administer Covid-19 vaccines during a global pandemic.

Lesson: President Trump is a lesson in how a leader gets branded by enemies and then acts in ways that confirm the branding is true

1. **The Necessaries**: The government was not ready for a pandemic. Trump acted quickly and decisively, directing resources to manage the right issues to keep hospitals supplied. There is a tendency to try to do a little of everything to avoid making a mistake in issues management. This usually overextends resources and slows down the process. The bigger the issue, the more focused and decisive actions must be. Making the best choice and going all-in is best practice in crisis when time matters.

2. **Playing a Losing Hand**: Trump's initial response was to say that everything was under control and that the virus would go away. On the surface this seemed naïve and dishonest. Trump had no cards to play. The choice was not between telling the truth, Covid-19 is a killer, and we can't stop it, or assuring people that we have it under control. Arguably, telling the truth would have terrified America resulting in panic. In issues management, sometimes you need to buy more time by saying or doing what is necessary to keep everything from unraveling before you are prepared to implement your plan.

3. **Credibility**: Trump had low approval. Many Americans thought he was a Russian agent. He had been impeached at the start of

Covid-19 in January 2020. He had been branded as racist in the press. He had ongoing battles with the media. His role in managing this crisis had to consider that reality. Issues management is not always a top-down endeavor. Sometimes it is best for the boss to operate behind the scenes and not be the public face. Trump had good management instincts, but he was not a scientist or a medical doctor.

4. **Environmental Scan**: Trump should have known that most in the press would give him no quarter. He would own every mistake. Democrats were poised to use his mistakes to their political advantage. In issues management, assessing your allies, enemies, weaknesses, and strengths at the start is vital to your success. Crisis makes you vulnerable and emboldens your opposition.

5. **Message Discipline**: The information that President Trump and his team would present throughout the Covid-19 crisis was extremely complex and nuanced. Scientific certainty is rare, and science is incomprehensible to most people. Scientific disagreement is commonplace. This created a challenge for message discipline because the virus was mutating, and new challenges were constantly emerging. In issues management you will sometimes face a rapidly evolving crisis. Often the key here is not to drill down too deeply on specifics. Keep it general. Paint in broad brushstrokes. Limit your public exposure. Going all in only to have things change leaves you with a lot to unpack. In issues management, complexity mixed with uncertainty is exceedingly difficult to manage.

6. **Loyalty**: The more difficult the crisis, the more important it is to surround yourself with people whose loyalty is unquestioned. There are always other agendas in play. One of the first jobs of the issues manager is to convince the team to suspend their personal goals until the crisis has been abated. Trump was dealing with both career and appointed consultants and advisers. Career people in government have a certain degree of immunity from doing what you want them to do. They are survivors. You have no real control over them. Realize this and act accordingly.

7. **Coordinate Resources**: Trump did an outstanding job at coordinating public and private resources to boost production and advance vaccine

discovery. Here his business experience served him well. In issues management, it is important that you know your organization's strengths and weaknesses. The skilled manager knows how to use team strengths and plug weaknesses. Match the right people with the demands of each task. This is the key skill to have in crisis management.

8. **Tame Bureaucracy**: Trump was not a huge fan of bureaucracy. It is slow. It is process driven. It is inflexible. This is not how you make money in business. Overhead is cost. He instinctively knew how things get from point "A" to point "B" and what questions to ask to find out what stood in the way of making things go faster. In "Operation Warp Speed," Trump tamed the bureaucracy. In issues management, it is important to know how your internal processes work. Crisis requires much faster response times. When developing your crisis plan, you should study your internal processes and ways you can improve response times. Bureaucratic decision-making can be your greatest enemy in a crisis.

9. **Outside Experts**: When you're getting a lot of the same advice, it is good practice to find other voices. Trump tapped Dr. Scott Atlas from Stanford University to be an informed second opinion on the science of the issue. Positioning an outside expert in issues management can be tricky. You need to avoid clashes with your incumbent professionals and turf battles. Handled poorly, outside professionals can disrupt alignment and undermine trust. In the worst case, outside experts can fragment your team into opposing camps. That is why it is important to have specific tasks for outside experts to perform.

10. **Stay in Your Wheelhouse**: In issues management, there should always be clear lines of responsibility that should not be crossed. It is rarely good practice to jump back and forth into spaces where you are not an expert. When a question is asked of an expert, avoid taking the microphone and try to answer it. Trump was the strategist, but he became too involved at the operational levels. Roles are particularly important in issues management. Credit will flow from success, and there is usually enough to go around. Wanting credit for everything usually costs you in the end.

11. **Limit Exposure**: The amount of public exposure should be determined by the nature of the issue. If flood waters are rising, then a

community will need to know the water levels in a timely manner. If a hurricane is coming ashore, then the community needs to follow its path in real time to prepare. As an issues manager, the question you always need to be asking is what news is there to report that is significant enough to move the needle. The only information that was constantly changing concerning Covid-19 every day was the number of cases. The painstaking analysis of these data did little to move the needle in Trump's favor. Franklin Roosevelt did only 30 fireside chats over a period of 11 plus years as president. President Trump had 25 briefings in less than six months on Covid-19. Too much of anything at some point backfires.

12. **Branding Overtakes Credibility**: Trump's negative branding turned what should have been a triumph into a loss. When he announced he would have a vaccine within a year, the press did not believe him and reported it as a boast. He did facilitate the creation and approval of two new vaccines within a year. There was no bounce for Trump from "Operation Warp Speed" even as the vaccines began to flow.

Chickens do come home to roost, and Trump's detractors and those who harbored ill will toward Trump came together to ensure that he would never get to spike the ball in the endzone to claim any credit for success in bringing new vaccines to market in record time. The Trump presidency is unique in that issues never much mattered. He did not rise or fall on his successes in domestic or foreign policy. He worked hard and got a whole lot done, but his persona was always the standard by which he was assessed.

He was a president who was genuinely loved by his supporters and viscerally hated by his enemies. In many ways, polling "approval versus disapproval" does not really capture his presidency. It was unique because his was the only presidency we covered in this book where the most significant issue was him. As Trump departed office, Gallup gave this assessment of his approval: "Trump is departing office having averaged 41 percent job approval during his four years in office, lower than any other president in Gallup polling history by four points."

Next up, we tackle our current president Joe Biden and explore how he is applying the lessons of issues management.

CHAPTER 16

Biden—Ignoring Issues

There is a proverb that states: "He loses his thanks who promises and delays." Delivering on expectations is critical to successful issues management. Joseph R. Biden, Jr. was elected to lower the temperature, quiet the noise, heal the nation, and end the scourge of Covid-19. Instead, he assumed the mandate to govern as a progressive—a mandate he never asked for and was never given permission to follow.

In January 2020, there was no pandemic. The economy was humming along. Trump seemed likely to be reelected. By the end of 2020, there would be 365,000 Americans reported dead with Covid-19. Also, on May 25, 2020, a man named George Floyd was forcibly restrained on the ground by a police officer's knee in Minneapolis, Minnesota, and he died. George Floyd was a Black man. An explosion of anger across the nation soon followed as protesters and rioters took to the streets.

These events would frame the presidential campaign in 2020—a contest in which the cultural, economic, and political differences between the two parties had never been greater. Then there was the wild card—Covid-19.

Biden had sought the presidency in 1988. That campaign became mired in accusations of plagiarism and exaggerated statements about his background. He dropped out. Although he explored other runs for president, he only ran again in 2008. He lost to Sen. Barack Obama but was selected as his vice president.

In 2020, Biden was neither a fresh face with innovative ideas nor widely viewed as a progressive. It could be argued that his ideas were out of step with most Democratic activists. He was also the oldest candidate in the field. As Covid-19 deaths rose, Trump was getting blamed, and he had no answers for ending the growing crisis except to wait for vaccines to be developed.

Biden did not run well in the early primaries and was viewed as all but finished when he left New Hampshire and headed for South Carolina. There was a debate there four days before the primary for Democratic candidates. Rep. Jim Clyburn, the most powerful Black elected official in the state, wanted to endorse his old friend Joe Biden, but he wanted something in return. As reported by NBC News, their conversation went this way, "You've had a couple of opportunities to mention naming a Black woman to the Supreme Court," Clyburn lectured his friend of nearly half a century, like a schoolteacher scolding a child. "I'm telling you, don't you leave the stage tonight without making it known that you will do that." Biden did what Clyburn asked when answering a question late in the debate with this response: "Everyone should be represented. The fact is, what we should be doing—we talked about the Supreme Court. I'm looking forward to making sure there's a Black woman on the Supreme Court…" The next day Clyburn endorsed Biden, and three days later, Biden won the South Carolina primary. With solid support in the Black community, Biden became the consensus candidate. Shortly thereafter, all but two of the remaining Democrats suspended their campaigns, setting up a race where Biden faced off against progressive Senators Bernie Sanders and Elizabeth Warren. Biden was conceded the entire ideological center of the Democratic Party resulting in him winning 46 contests, 51.8 percent of the primary vote, and 2,687 of the 3,979 delegates available.

In his acceptance speech at the Democratic convention Joe Biden:

1. **Addressed Divisions**: "Too much anger, too much fear, too much division. Here and now I give you my word. If you entrust me with the presidency, I will draw on the best of us, not the worst. I will be an ally of the light, not the darkness. It is time for us, for we, the people, to come together. And make no mistake, united we can and will overcome this season of darkness in America."

2. **Claimed the Middle**: "I will be an American president. I'll work hard for those who didn't support me, as hard for them as I did for those who did vote for me. That's the job of a president, to represent all of us, not just our base or our party. This is not a partisan moment. This must be an American moment."

3. **Defined the Challenge**: "Four, four historic crises all at the same time: a perfect storm. The worst pandemic in over 100 years, the worst economic crisis since the great depression, the most compelling call for racial justice since the '60s and the undeniable realities and just the accelerating threats of climate change. So, the question for us is simple: Are we ready? I believe we are. We must be."

4. **Stated the Choice**: "Character is on the ballot. Compassion is on the ballot. Decency, science, democracy. They're all on the ballot. Who we are as a nation, what we stand for, and most importantly, who we want to be, that's all on the ballot? And the choice could not be clearer. No rhetoric is needed."

According to Gallup, Trump's approval rating between July and October 2020 averaged around 42 percent. One finding from the October poll proved to be prophetic:

> The poll finds an improvement in Americans' satisfaction with the way things are going in the United States—to 19 percent from 14 percent in September. The current satisfaction rating remains well below the historical average of 36 percent. It is similar to the levels Gallup measured around the time of the 1980 and 1992 presidential elections that saw incumbents Jimmy Carter and George H.W. Bush defeated for a second term in office. The lowest satisfaction recorded in a year when an incumbent was reelected was 33 percent in 2012.

Joe Biden spent a large part of his campaign at his home in Delaware because of concerns about Covid-19. Voters understood. His strategy was to allow Trump to be the aggressor and punch himself out. The political translation is that he would frustrate Trump into making mistakes and unforced errors. Biden spokesman Matt Hill, as reported in TIME, framed it this way, "People are in pain. They've lost their jobs and their loved ones. And they're looking for an experienced and empathetic leader who can unite, heal, and move this country forward."

The 2020 election would be the largest turnout election in history. Biden would get 81.2 million votes and Trump 74.2 million, both were the highest totals ever by a candidate of their respective political party. In the end, Biden won 306 electoral votes to Trump's 232. Trump would claim the election was stolen and continue the fight through state and federal courts where he repeatedly lost. Trump's claims of a "stolen election" would crescendo on January 6, 2021, when Trump supporters breached the capitol building in protest. This would send Trump's approval plummeting downward as he headed into his post-presidency.

In Biden's inaugural address on January 20, 2021, he delivered:

1. **Call for Unity**: "So now, on this hallowed ground where just days ago violence sought to shake this Capitol's very foundation, we come together as one nation, under God, indivisible, to carry out the peaceful transfer of power as we have for more than two centuries."

2. **The Challenge**: "And now, a rise in political extremism, white supremacy, domestic terrorism that we must confront and we will defeat. To overcome these challenges—to restore the soul and to secure the future of America—requires more than words. It requires that most elusive of things in a democracy."

3. **Framed His Cause**: "Uniting to fight the common foes we face: Anger, resentment, hatred. Extremism, lawlessness, violence. Disease, joblessness, hopelessness. With unity we can do great things. Important things."

4. **Delivered His Promise**: "And together, we shall write an American story of hope, not fear. Of unity, not division. Of light, not darkness. An American story of decency and dignity. Of love and of healing. Of greatness and of goodness."

This was the message Americans expected from the healer they had elected. His first actions painted a slightly different picture. On his first day in office, Biden used executive orders to shut down the Keystone Pipeline, stop construction on Trump's border wall, and direct a whole-of-government approach toward achieving racial equity. In a nation still recovering from four years of political division, these actions were not designed to reverse this trend.

Biden, as America would discover, did not see himself simply as a healer of a broken nation and a Covid-19 fighter. He envisioned himself as an aspirational president, determined to conduct a consequential presidency. His presidential role model was Franklin Roosevelt, and he saw himself as the kind of transformational figure that Roosevelt was. He also believed that like Lyndon Johnson, whose "Great Society" programs expanded the social safety net, he could enact major legislative initiatives that would "reset America." His program was named "Build Back Better."

Biden would meet with historians at an undisclosed meeting in the White House in March 2021 to discuss "how big is too big—and how fast is too fast—to jam through once-in-a-lifetime historic changes to America." The advice he got: "It is time to go even bigger and faster than anyone expected. If that means chucking the filibuster and bipartisanship, so be it." Axios reported that an attitude of "think big—go big" pervaded the West Wing of the White House. Its reporting continued that the meeting was organized by historian Jon Meacham and included Doris Kearns Goodwin, Michael Beschloss, author Michael Eric Dyson, Yale's Joanne Freeman, Princeton's Eddie Glaude Jr., Harvard's Annette Gordon-Reed, and Walter Isaacson. Biden wanted to use the Covid-19 crisis as the springboard from which to enact systemic changes to America's society and economy. The recommendations of the panel persuaded Biden that a fundamental reset of America was indicated.

The idea for a "Great Reset" is not one Biden and his team created. The World Economic Forum (WEF), that hosts global elites and business and world leaders each year at meetings in Davos, Switzerland, is a forum on global issues. Recently, the meeting focused on what the world would look like post-capitalism. Many of the papers and discussions at the forum saw the global pandemic as a launch point to rethink global economics and global governance.

On the WEF website is this statement about the new world order:

> To achieve a better outcome, the world must act jointly and swiftly to revamp all aspects of our societies and economies, from education to social contracts and working conditions. Every country, from the United States to China, must participate, and every industry, from oil and gas to tech, must be transformed. In short, we need a "Great Reset" of capitalism.

Components of WEF's plan are listed in this order:

The first would steer the market toward fairer outcomes ... The second would ensure that investments advance shared goals, such as equality and sustainability ... The final priority would harness the innovations of the Fourth Industrial Revolution to support the public good, especially by addressing health and social challenges.

The agenda is a form of hybrid-socialism, tied to the "green" agenda, powered by hardship and division, and focused on achieving universal equity. There is one other term that came straight out of the WEF that has been adopted by the Biden team—Build Back Better.

Arguably there are three Biden personas. The first is "Senator Biden," who was a team player in the U.S. Senate for 36 years. His positions were mostly slightly left of center. This is the persona he ran on and won the presidency. The second image, which is widely debated, is "Progressive Biden." This posits Biden lurched far left after becoming president to appease the progressive wing of his party. Early in his presidency, President Biden has been closer to the views held by Senator Bernie Sanders than to those of moderate Senator Joe Manchin. The third persona is "Transformational Biden." Here Biden is focused on achieving greatness along the lines of an FDR presidency using the "Great Reset" as his roadmap.

The world does not stay in place while you pursue your goals. Issues are constantly evolving. A president can only focus on a few things, but he must be aware of many other issues to make sure problems do not become crises. There were a lot of problems that got worse early in the Biden administration. The withdrawal from Afghanistan lacked a cohesive exit strategy and damaged our standing in the world. The southern border grew more chaotic and unable to be managed. Inflation outpaced wage growth leaving 57 percent of Americans living paycheck to paycheck. Crime ran rampant in many cities while police were defunded, and criminals were freed back on to the streets. Homelessness grew out of control in many large cities. Deadly illegal drugs like fentanyl were crossing the border and killing Americans in larger numbers. The public school system was failing to measure up in reading and mathematics proficiency.

The national debt continued growing larger each year. Recruitment goals were not being met for our military.

As an issues manager, problems can easily negate successes. The impression that you are taking one step forward and two steps backward does not help sustain momentum. This is not to say that Biden did not accomplish key goals. He passed The American Rescue Plan extending Covid-19 relief, provided $1.2 trillion in his Infrastructure Investment and Jobs Act, and passed a $500 billion Inflation Reduction Act. The problem is that that these big things did little to broaden his base of support or sustain his momentum. Big things are great to accomplish, but they do not pay dividends quickly.

In his first few years, Biden has done several really big things, but in several areas, he has been tripped up by the issues he has ignored. These mistakes have hurt his support and given the impression that the nation is on the wrong track.

Lessons

At Issue: President Biden has pursued his goal of creating a green economy without a clear mandate and to the exclusion of addressing several other pressing issues.

Lesson: Ignoring issues, even when they are not your top priorities, can derail your strategy.

1. **Big Tent**: Biden's goals to transform the economy with renewable energy and bridge the racial divide would have been so much easier to achieve had he spent more time healing the nation. Division is toxic to effective issues management. The border wall had nothing to do with these goals, but shutting it down helped created two new issues: mass migration and fentanyl that hurt his momentum. Solutions that create new problems are not wise because they take the focus off what you are trying to accomplish and compete with your narrative.

2. **Mandate**: Americans thought they had hired a healer, unifier, and someone to end the scourge of Covid-19 when electing Joe Biden president. Instead, Biden's administration has focused on economic transformation by transitioning to renewable energy. You do not

need a mandate to carry out your agenda, but it is good practice to blend into your plan. President Obama did not have a mandate for Obamacare, but he managed the issue effectively with limited blow-back. Shutting down the Keystone Pipeline did not send a concil-iatory message, but rather it deepened the political divide. It would have been much better to position fossil fuels as transitional until the green economy is ready. Again, this move created problems not only for drivers with high gas prices but internationally for nations that depend on fossil fuels.

3. **Momentum**: Biden focused on undoing several Trump initiatives, some of which were working. This is a gamble in issues management because you are being reactive rather than proactive and creating conflict unnecessarily. Successful issues managers build momentum. As a leader, you do not undo the work of your predecessor because you can. You build on it, improve it, and integrate your priorities into it. There are so many problems that can be created when clear-ing the slate, and you will own them. It can really hurt your credibil-ity, so give it a lot of thought and try not to act in haste.

4. **Ignoring Problems**: The rationale for all issues management is shap-ing a problem so it does not grow into a crisis. Having your priorities does not make other issues disappear. Crossing the goal line and scor-ing one touchdown usually does not win the game, so do not shut down other issues while you focus on your priorities. Crime, inflation, and an open southern border are all real issues in the minds of the American people. Giving the appearance of ignoring or downplaying them undermines a leader's ability to align people behind his priorities. In May 2022, Pew Research found 70 percent of Americans thought inflation was a "very big problem," while 57 percent viewed climate change as a moderate or lesser problem. The leader needs to be viewed as not ignoring problems that are very real to people. As an issues man-ager, understanding this point is particularly important.

5. **Planning**: Plans need to be skillfully created and artfully presented to show that you understand the problem and that your approach will create the desired results. The absence of planning is chaos. You want to avoid being perceived as not having an actionable plan to manage other things when you undertake big things. The Biden

administration's hasty withdrawal from Afghanistan seemed to have a goal without an actionable plan behind it, resulting in poor sequencing of tactics. There is another good lesson here. Americans wanted the withdrawal of troops from Afghanistan, but they wanted it done correctly without the loss of American lives and damage to America's standing in the world. The lesson here is that effective issues management goes beyond achieving a consensus goal. It must be done correctly.

6. **Crisis**: When an issue grows into a crisis on your watch, then you own it. The southern border has been a problem for decades. Congress has failed to act to pass comprehensive immigration reform. President Biden inherited a border that was secure, and processes for dealing with migrants were working, but for how long? As an issues manager, this is a ticking time bomb. The only question is when it is going to explode. The issues manager does not want to be blamed for a problem he did not create. Taking unilateral actions transfers both authority and responsibility to you. Keep as many safeguards in place for as long as you can while you bring as many people under the tent as possible to work on a comprehensive solution. The rule is to leave what is working alone until you have developed a replacement plan that works better. By stopping the wall, that some viewed as working, Biden transferred all responsibility for what happened going forward to himself.

7. **Support**: Levels of support change throughout an issues life. What you want to avoid are actions that drive your levels of support downward for a prolonged period. Try to avoid making it too difficult for others to follow your lead by making the price of support too high or too perilous. To use a baseball analogy, if you want fans in the stands, then there is a very simple formula—win. To keep them in the stands—keep winning. President Biden's failure to gain momentum early cost him public support in the polls. A few quick victories, like FDR did with the bank holiday, would have become a launch point and opened the door to doing bigger things. In issues management, you always need to walk before you run. The importance of early success far outpaces the setting of lofty goals in contributing to your success.

8. **Lower the Temperature**: In issues management, the leader must be agile and willing to change as circumstances warrant and resources permit. Biden inherited a very discordant issue—vaccine rollout. This was the most challenging issue he faced because it was so divisive. You can't force a horse to drink, and punishment usually does not produce desired results. This issue required engagement skills and patience. It was not a "check the box" issue. Acknowledge that the fear and concerns are real to those who have them. Broaden your base of advocates. Remember, you do not get a second chance to set the tone, so it is important to modulate when needed. Another lesson is to make sure that you are positioned properly when the issue changes. Most people under Biden got vaccinated and boosted once, then the virus changed, and support naturally waned. The response to change needs to be immediate. Stay in step with the issue and tack with the shifts.

9. **When and When Not to Intervene**: Careful judgment is required by a president in determining when and when not to intervene. One key in issues management is not to create enemies who would have no reason to oppose you. One of the most politically divisive issues that arose in Biden's first few years in office was the teaching of Critical Race Theory in schools. Few cultural issues divided the political parties more than this one. Another was gender affirming care. Biden was faced with the dilemma of weighing in on these issues or refraining from doing so. Should he express his own beliefs and the beliefs of the majority of those who elected him and, in doing so, appear to ignore the sentiments of those who did not, many of whom held opposing beliefs? Or should he refrain from doing so? Biden chose to weigh in, but in doing so, suffered the consequences of appearing to have intervened where he had nothing to gain. In the larger sense, you do not want to start a fight with your customers, who in this case were mostly suburban parents, many of whom voted for Biden. Quickly identify issues that provide you with nothing to gain.

10. **Starting Line**: Ideally, successful issues management should build and strengthen your base of support. Anything you do that results in a loss of support will require time, effort, and resources to get you back to the starting line. Biden's poor issues management, in the

examples I have cited and others, has cost him support from Democrats, Hispanics, and Independents. Much of this is a result of how he managed the issues he prioritized and issues he chose to ignore. In issues management, every action has a price tag attached to it. The skilled issues manager sees it quickly.

11. **Resurgence**: Americans are a forgiving people, and we are a nation of second chances. The beauty of issues management is that the field of play is always changing, and your next success can change the entire conversation. In issues management, change is the only constant. Events alter and reframe issues. The challenge for the Biden team will be to learn from mistakes made and apply the rules of successful issues management going forward.

As this chapter ends, President Biden has declared his candidacy for reelection. He is traveling the country selling his economic plan, that he has branded "Bidenomics." Seventy-four percent of the American people think that the country is on the "wrong track." These are not only Republicans or Trump supporters. There is a portion of this perception that stems from how Biden managed issues.

In the last chapter, as an issues manager, I want to review lessons learned.

CHAPTER 17

Final Thoughts

Professor Albert Einstein captures the essence of issues management with this observation about problem solving: "We cannot solve problems with the kind of thinking we employed when we came up with them." It is incumbent upon the leader to understand the issue that needs to be solved in its proper context leaving prejudgment at the door.

Organizationally, the leader's job is to develop and implement a comprehensive strategy, organize resources operationally, and implement a plan of action with tactical agility. This requires intelligence, agility, adaptability, effective communication, organizational skills, and, in most situations, courage.

President Theodore Roosevelt said: "At any moment of decision, the best thing to do is the right thing, the next best thing is the wrong thing, and the worst thing you can do is nothing." The caution here is to remember activity is not a strategy. Making a mistake when carrying out a well-conceived strategy is vastly different from stumbling along when you have no clearly defined goals or plan of action. The purpose of action is to create momentum toward achieving a solution—period.

Professor Michael Porter wrote: "The essence of strategy is choosing what not to do." Obviously, you cannot do everything, but trying to do more than is needed wastes time and resources. This lesson was taught by President Johnson, who passed the most ambitious social agenda since FDR before stubbornly pursuing victory in Vietnam at any cost. There is often the temptation to put one more ball in the air. Avoid it whenever possible to steer clear of mission creep.

Strategy provides you with a true north and helps to keep you focused and on track as things change. Assessing operationally provides inventory of assets and personnel to uncover gaps in organizational capabilities while you still have time to do something about it. President Kennedy had a plan for the Bay of Pigs, but he did not question whether assets were strategically aligned to achieve success. This would precipitate failure because of mistakes early in the implementation of the plan.

In issues management, controlling the narrative creates positive momentum. This helped Franklin Roosevelt convert doubters and fence sitters into supporters. Helping your stakeholders understand what you are doing, why you are doing it, and what they can expect in terms of results is key to building and maintaining support.

Proper sequencing of activities is key to successful rollout of your plan. Moving to action too quickly to get results can create false readings of progress that can result in one step forward and two steps back.

The cadence of issues management is problem—strategy—action—assessment—action—result. The best practice is making this happen on an established timeline. President Clinton wanted universal health care. He assigned First Lady Hillary Clinton to develop the plan. He wanted the plan in 100 days. It was late. The process was secretive. There was little opportunity provided for outside buy-in. By the time the proposal was presented, other issues had become priorities. The lesson here is the bigger the issue, the tighter the process needs to be, and the more important it becomes.

Proper alignment of people, resources, and information are factors that lead to success. The team needs to be carefully chosen to assemble the necessary skills sets. Let strategy be your guide in creating your team. President Eisenhower was masterful at alignment when managing school desegregation in Little Rock, Arkansas. His use of force was measured and justified. He engaged but did not create a "win-lose" outcome with the governor of Arkansas. He lowered the temperature and drew a line in the sand that sent a fair warning to anyone else who wanted to challenge the primacy of federal power to enforce school desegregation. And he created a framework to manage the issue going forward.

Power relationships are not always equal. Having power does not give you the authority to do whatever you want is a valuable lesson. President George W. Bush was commander-in-chief of the armed forces of the United States. He had the power to commit troops into conflict but did not have the "authority" to topple governments or build nations. In issues management, you will be tempted to go beyond your mandate to pursue new opportunities or solve other problems. It is usually best to avoid this temptation. President Bush forgot to define victory clearly and fell victim to mission creep.

Peter Drucker said: "The most important thing in communication is to hear what isn't being said." This is a great skill to have as a leader. Great leaders solicit and heed the advice of others. They also can effectively read people to pick up on the nuances of what is not being said. Keep your door open and encourage members of your team to speak freely. Reward honesty and objective appraisal and make it clear that you do not appreciate team members holding back information. President Trump was seen by his detractors as undisciplined and accountable to only himself. His actions at the Covid-19 press conferences served only to support this belief. Try to avoid a situation where team members are afraid to approach you, question bad decisions, or believe you will not listen to them.

Controlling the narrative is equivalent to the military strategy of taking the high ground. As a leader you need a narrative that is robust, understandable, and sustainable. The components of the narrative are the story, audience, and filters. The process involves developing strategic content, message consistency, timely delivery, effective targeting, and exploring all available channels to expand your reach. Roosevelt in his first term enjoyed complete message dominance. This was not an accident but rather the result of having a clear vision for his presidency and using radio effectively. President Obama established a social media presence that enabled him to communicate without filters during his first presidential campaign. This served him well throughout his presidency. The worst position is having nothing new to say or no one left to listen. This is what happened to President Johnson on Vietnam.

Internal communications requires that you identify key stakeholders and properly segment your audience so that the right message is being delivered to the most receptive recipients. It is also important to open channels to receive feedback which is a straightforward way to gather intelligence about how your plan is being perceived. Externally, a major challenge is finding the right images and voices to communicate your message. Here you can "borrow" the goodwill of opinion and community leaders to drive a message because they have established trust. President Trump was a highly effective communicator to his base, but his opponents saw through a completely different lens and tuned out. This shifted focus from the issues he managed to his personal traits and motivations. Avoid having your motivations questioned by others.

Issues managers also need a plan for effective outreach and engagement. In World War II, the big guns on ships and bombs delivered by aircraft softened up the enemy, but it did not eliminate the need for ground troops to take and hold territory. In issues management, communications help to create a more favorable environment for your issue, but it often takes grassroots engagement and outreach to change hearts and minds. The difference between Presidents Kennedy and Johnson legislatively was the personal relationships Johnson had cultivated. What produced far different outcomes in Watergate versus Iran-Contra with Nixon and Reagan was Reagan's reservoir of goodwill. What sank Trump in the end was he did not embrace the adage: "Your friends don't elect you; your enemies defeat you." Too many of his options were seen as "win-lose" by his opponents.

The last component is the need to produce measurable results. This is where the pursuit of your goals is matched to the coordination and alignment of internal capabilities with fully integrated resources sequenced to achieve successful outcomes. President George H.W. Bush led an international coalition to oust the forces of Saddam Hussein from Kuwait. His objective was clear, and when it was accomplished, he stopped prosecuting the war. This is a critical lesson in issues management: When you win—stop solving the problem.

There are 10 steps in issues management:

1. **Frame the Issue**: An honest assessment of what lies at the root of the problem is required. This is never easy and is sometimes unpleasant. Avoid the "we have to do something" approach to issue framing, because it can lead to a premature reaction. Take the time you need to get it right. Remember the words of Albert Einstein: "If I had an hour to solve a problem I'd spend 55 minutes thinking about the problem and five minutes thinking about solutions."

2. **Define Success**: At the very beginning the leader should define what a successful outcome looks like. Success comes in many forms. Sometimes success is lowering the heat, removing obstacles to progress,

aligning operations, or putting in place processes that will resolve issues down the road. Whatever your defined outcome is, remember that when you have achieved it, the process ends.

3. **Define Limits**: Actions need to have parameters attached to them. Great leaders understand the limits of their power. Quality issues management requires leadership, but no one can do it alone. Zig Zigler said: "You don't build a business—you build people—and then people build your business." Applied to issues management it would read: "You don't manage the issue alone—you build a team—and they solve the problem with you."

4. **Create a Strategy**: Strategy is what gets you from where you are to where you need to be. In all issues management the playing field is constantly changing. This means that most plans will not be followed exactly as drawn up, but this does not dilute the fact that you did plan and have pieces on the board ready to move, albeit not in the way you originally intended. Part of the planning process should anticipate moves that could be made by the opposition and prepare the appropriate responses that give you a clear advantage in establishing and maintaining positive momentum toward achieving the goals you have set.

5. **Align Resources**: John D. Rockefeller advocated doing the common things "uncommonly well." This is good advice for issues managers because any flaw in operational alignment or tactical execution will be quickly revealed. Remember, as soon as you start executing everything accelerates. You will not have time to align key people and resources on the run. Key to success is having the right people in position, information organized, and a workable plan in place.

6. **First Move—Right Move**: You want decisive action at the beginning to build momentum. This will allow you to properly sequence the tactics that follow. Do not be afraid to be bold. President Theodore Roosevelt said it best: "The only man who never makes mistakes is the man who never does anything." Make every effort to assure your first move counts, but also avoid overanalyzing the issue, which can lead to inaction, at which point events can overwhelm you.

7. **Assess Twice—Act Once**: There is often the "fog of war" where it is difficult to accurately assess the results of your actions in real

time. This is why we suggest a review of tactics whenever possible. I have always liked this quote from Alvin Toffler to broaden this point: "You've got to think about big things while you're doing small things, so that all the small things go in the right direction." The process will inundate you with data and information, so always keep the big picture front and center. This helps you from getting lost in the details.

8. **Accept the Outcome**: Success is not guaranteed. A leader can do everything right and still end up falling short of creating a positive outcome. Not all issues can be successfully managed. It is important that in the end that you accept the outcome, learn from it, and then move on. Avoid the "would have, should have and could have" assessment pitfalls. Focus on outcomes achieved and changes that need to be made to move forward.

9. **Learn from the Experience**: The process by its nature brings change with it. These changes can help your organizations advance to the next level or force you to reexamine long-held beliefs that did not hold up under pressure. In each case they should not be ignored. As the leader, it is up to you to understand the lessons that each project generates and use them to advance or to help rethink your organization going forward.

10. **Manage Change**: The evolution of the leader is to move from the issues manager to the change manager after the process ends. Embrace the challenge. Many on your team will grow during the experience when given the opportunity to take the initiative, while for others, the effort will serve to highlight some deficiencies. Build off both.

Let us end by revisiting one lesson in issues management we can take from each of the 15 presidents we have examined in this book:

ROOSEVELT: He teaches us that momentum is gained by having a clear focus, asking for permission, clearly defining objectives, and getting people to buy-in to your vision. Roosevelt is a great case study in how to build momentum behind change.

TRUMAN: The lesson here is you are never sure of the challenges you will face. Big decisions end up in the lap of the leader and they do not have a manual attached. It is up to the leader to assess the pluses and minuses and do what is best. This is not a popularity contest. Make the best choice available, be willing to accept the consequences, and move on.

EISENHOWER: It takes a lot of skill to transform a big problem into a smaller, more manageable one. A skilled issues manager, who fully understands the problem, will be able to assess the components of the problem to find the optimal path toward a solution. Effective issues management is often about solving a lot of small issues rather than tackling the large, more obvious ones. Eisenhower created the "win-win" outcome that provided future direction to issues managers.

KENNEDY: Failure, framed in the proper context, is not a complete failure. The Bay of Pigs was a failure, but when Kennedy addressed the American people, he presented a new world order where nuclear powers no longer fight conventional wars. This did not erase his failure but made the action he took more justifiable. In issues management, actions need an understandable rationale. Actions should have logical foundations so you can move on to the next steps and justify failure in pursuit of valid objectives.

JOHNSON: He teaches the power of relationships in getting things done. Johnson's "Great Society" initiatives were all enacted into law because Johnson had done the spadework with Congress long in advance of the ask. A successful issues manager builds on the relationships cultivated over time and builds political capital.

NIXON: He teaches us that issues left unattended become crises and that your power and position cannot protect you from shifts in public opinion. When confronted with a crisis, the worst thing a leader can do is believe that no one will care, or it will go away. In issues management, once you allow others to frame the issue, you lose control of the narrative. You never want to be playing catch up when managing a crisis.

FORD: Here we learn that doing what you perceive to be the right thing is not always rewarded. Ford pardoned Nixon to help the nation heal. In issues management, the proper sequence of activities provides proper context for action. There were important steps that Ford missed, the most important of which was reassuring the American people that he had put rules in place to make sure that Watergate would never happen again. By not doing this, he opened the door to criticism that the pardon was political.

CARTER: Taking a strategic pause is not always a good idea. Activity builds on activity, and when you stop advancing, you lose momentum. Also, by Carter putting his presidency on hold over the hostage crisis, he was drawing attention to his failure. Carter did not sufficiently weigh the fact that the hostage takers were given control of the issue by his decision. There was nothing to be gained by waiting for the hostage takers to accede to his demand. They would wait and release the hostages on the day Ronald Reagan was sworn-in as president, which was tantamount to one last slap on the face.

REAGAN: He shows us resilience. Reagan's first two years in office were not successful in terms of quickly turning around the economy, but he was not deterred. He kept moving forward, believing that his policies were right for America and would accomplish the objectives he had promised. The hardest thing to balance in issues management is whether to stay the course or adjust strategy to meet immediate demands for action. This is when it is always helpful to measure your leash to see how much you have left. There is a world of difference between being suborn and wrong and being persistent and right.

BUSH 41: Here we learn that problems do not disappear, they simply move on to the next person. Bush had to deal with the fallout of Iran-Contra after he became president because the issues did not disappear when Reagan left office. As you assume leadership, always survey the playing field to determine what you have inherited. Take the bow for the "win-win." Closely monitor the fallout from "win-lose." Be ready to act decisively to benefit from the "lose-win." Lastly, assess the damage inflicted from "lose-lose" and turn the page as quickly as possible.

CLINTON: Always be willing to adapt to changing circumstances. Unlike Reagan, Clinton folded his hand after a devastating defeat in the midterm elections. In issues management, a lot of times, we make assumptions that are wrong, and we need to correct them. Clinton miscalculated the American public's appetite for expansive government. He could have stuck to his guns and lost power in 1996, but instead, he changed course and went on to have a successful presidency.

BUSH 43: Events destroy plans. As a former governor, President Bush planned to focus on education. The attacks on 9/11 thrust him into being a wartime president. This was not an easy transition to make. He had to go back to the drawing board and craft a new strategy to deal with a new issue. He had to realign internal resources by creating the Department of Homeland Security and shift away from his domestic focus. In issues management, sometimes the environment changes dramatically and has nothing to do with you, but you must deal with the consequences. These are the moments when leadership is not an option. Embrace them.

OBAMA: His greatest success, Affordable Care Act, teaches us the value of learning from the mistake of others. In the Book of Ecclesiastes 1:9, it is written: "What has been will be again, what has been done will be done again; there is nothing new under the sun." Obama learned valuable lessons in issues management from the failure of Hillary Clinton in 1993. The main lesson was to invite the skeptical to join you under the tent. In issues management, friends and enemies are often fungible as alliances often shift within the process of an issue's evolution. Keep your door always open and your ear to the ground to respond appropriately when change comes.

TRUMP: Here we learn the limitations of imposing your will. Trump gave the American people a simple choice that you are either with me or I am against you. He drew a very clear line between friends and enemies. Success at issues management requires the leader to be tactful, diplomatic, sensible, discreet, flexible, and practical. Sometimes you will ruffle a few feathers, but this should be more strategic than deliberate. Trump's style created enemies not adversaries. It is important in issues management to understand that today's adversary may be tomorrow's ally and that the enemy of my enemy is my friend. Alliances and loyalties can always shift, so factor that into your strategy.

BIDEN: Biden pursued a transformational agenda around climate and equity without a clear mandate. He did not follow the rules on issues management like setting clear goals and using initial successes to create momentum for the really big things you want to do. He also created enemies by allowing crises to develop by ignoring issues that impacted peoples' lives like inflation and crime. In issues management, there is always the need to reconcile what you would like to accomplish with the reality of your situation. In every project, you have limited political capital and resources at your disposal. A good plan will guide you in using resources wisely, efficiently, and effectively.

As president you need to accept that you will not be able to do everything you set out to accomplish and that the unexpected is the ordinary. Presidents are shaped by how well they managed issues during the times in which they served. Every president managed complex issues, and each tried to do the best he could to serve the American people, but some fell short of our expectations.

Thank you for joining me on this journey. I hope that you enjoyed it and learned something along the way.

Epilogue

As I finished writing this book, I was working on a strategic positioning project for an association client. Many of the lessons contained in this book were applied in helping the client set goals, develop strategy, optimize resources, secure buy-in, and define the organization's functional capabilities. The objective was to better position the organization to successfully meet the challenges posed by shifts in the social and political climate over the next three years.

Like Roosevelt, the leader asked for input and permission from his Board members to scale and develop the strategy. We called on Truman when a difficult decision between two alternatives had to be made and neither was without risks. Eisenhower provided guidance when pairing down big issues into more actionable parts. Kennedy provided caution to reexamine each piece of our action plans to make sure they were supported before moving forward.

The client had to call on the goodwill he had established with his Board when making the tough calls, thank you to President Johnson. We weighted each issue to properly sequence activity. President Nixon provided us with the valuable lesson to address problems early before they become crises. We focused goals that advanced the organization's value proposition and did not become entangled in other issues that would have side-tracked us, thank you President Ford.

Taking a lesson from President Carter, we did not try to change what we could not control. Throughout the process, we remained optimistic and committed to key goals we had established and our working set of assumptions about the environment in which the plan would be implemented, much like President Reagan's belief in his course of action. President Bush 41 provided cautions that when you set an objective and reach it, then declare victory and move on. We applied a lesson from President Clinton when we met stiff resistance from stakeholders and adjusted course in order to move forward.

President Bush 43 provided guidance that we must operate within established parameters and not arbitrarily expand boundaries because new opportunities were revealed during the process. President Obama informed our thinking when doing an environmental scan to look closely at what worked and what failed in the past and incorporate it into our planning. We also made our tent as big as possible to expand our stakeholder base and welcome input. President Trump's experiences alerted us not to make the process about personalities but rather stick to the issues and assess them with transparency and credibility. We applied a lesson of President Biden when choosing our path forward in putting stakeholder expectations first and foremost. We delivered what we promised to accomplish.

It is my hope that the leader who reads this book will apply the lessons contained in this book when addressing issues and problem-solving within your organization. I have always found it much easier to remember what a president did than try to recall something I read in a college textbook or heard in a lecture hall.

My second hope is that university professors see the book as a cross-disciplinary resource and supplemental reading for classes in management, leadership communications, and public relations. In management, the lessons provide examples of decision-making, planning, organizing, and assessment. The examples provided on strategy, change management, and disruption can all be studied in leadership classes. The value of how we communicate to key stakeholders is clearly shown by several of the presidents we reviewed and can be integrated into a communications curriculum. And the concepts of strategic communications and crisis management are evident in every chapter for those learning about public relations and public affairs.

Lastly, I hope that the book will help in some way to provide a foundation on which to build a more civil discourse in our politics. Assessing an elected official on issues management skills rather than party affiliation, philosophy, or where they fit on some arbitrary political spectrum lowers the temperature while encouraging rigorous debate.

When a politician starts talking tactics before providing a rationale for why an action needs to be taken, then questions need to be asked and answered. Activity has never been a substitute for strategy, yet too many people believe that spending money is a strategy unto itself. We need problems solved, and the presidents we have examined in this book have provided us with valuable lessons in successful issues management and lessons we can learn from failure to manage an issue. Asking a person to clearly define goals and results sought is not questioning their motivations but rather requesting the person articulate anticipated results before acting, then holding the person accountable.

As I finish this book, the United States is helping Ukraine militarily fight Russia. As an issues manager, I see two questions that were not asked or answered: What does victory look like, and can we get a better peace deal in two years than we can get today? The strategy in Ukraine has been open checkbook and as long as it takes. When you lead with a promise of limitless resources without clear goals attached, you risk ending up on the short end of the stick, because you have inadvertently assumed responsibility for what happens going forward. This means that the United States is positioned to be blamed for any failure due to insufficient resources at the time and place they were needed. When you make open-ended promises, then you surrender control of the process. This is not the best issues management practice.

Lastly, I want to stress that my analysis of the issues presented should be viewed as the starting line rather than an end point. The goal was to present examples to show the process at work. Feel free to add other facts and data and to reach your own conclusions.

As a business tool, supplemental reading for course work or catalyst to promote more open and civil political discussions, my hope is that you find this simple work, and the lessons contained within it, useful and helpful.

About the Author

Dennis M. Powell has spent his career making complex information understandable as a consultant, author, writer, presenter, and educator. As a consultant, he focuses on strategy development, resource alignment, and creating tactical agility to help his clients successfully manage complex issues. As a writer, he examines political and social trends and is an opinion contributor to The Hill, The Messenger, and Inside Sources. Mr. Powell has presented to national and statewide organizations on issues management best practices and social and political trends as well as conducted training and workshops for established and aspiring leaders. He was host of a nationally syndicated radio program where he interviewed business leaders and entrepreneurs.

Index

www.ingramcontent.com/pod-product-compliance
Lightning Source LLC
Chambersburg PA
CBHW061213220326
41599CB00025B/4630